D1366404

COPYRIGHT NOTICE

Farm Fresh Books are available at special discounts for bulk purchases (shipping and handling charges apply). For more information, contact:

Farm Fresh Books
www.farmfreshbooks.com
(800) 891-0466

If you would like to contact the author for an interview or other publicity/media request, go to:
www.michaelturback.com

Book design by CObP Design, Ithaca, NY

Printed in the United States of America

The Finger Lakes is not the Mosel or Alsace, but the vines don't seem to care.

Contents

Contents

About the Author

As true a Finger Lakes zealot as there ever was and a locavore before the word existed, Michael Turback was among the first to embrace concepts of farm-to-table and vineyard-to-table at his restaurant, Turback's of Ithaca — an achievement recognized nationally. Michael not only created and nurtured one of the region's first destination restaurants, he built a reputation around his ability to stalk, procure, and support the best of local food and wine. *The Los Angeles Times* called Turback's, "the first Finger Lakes restaurant to really devote itself to New York's culinary and enological bounty."

Turback's was at the epicenter of the rebirth of wine culture in the region. Konstantin Frank, Guy DeVaux, Charles Fournier, and John Williams came to pour their wines. Walter Taylor would sit at the bar and sketch drawings for Bully Hill labels. André Tchelistcheff visited from California to see what all the fuss was about.

The restaurant's library of early vintages documented the progress of the growing local industry, earning attention and commendation from *The Wine Spectator, Bon Appetit, Gourmet Magazine, The New York Times, Boston Globe, Washington Post, Philadelphia Inquirer, USA Today, Wall Street Journal, Fortune Magazine, Nation's Restaurant News,* the Food Channel, and NPR's "All Things Considered." A true "local movement" pioneer, Michael's efforts sparked trends that are seen throughout the hospitality industry today. His loyalty to small local farmers and use of seasonal local produce helped to popularize American regional dining; his wine tasting events and wine dinners inspired interest in a new generation of regional wines. The Turback's staff even picked local grapes for the restaurant's house wine.

Michael originated "The Great Nouveau Race," in which long-distance runners carried each new vintage's first-released bottles of local wines to market, upstaging the arrival of Beaujolais Nouveau from France and nearly creating an international incident!

His restaurant's success discredited the prevailing snub of New York State wines by the experts and critics. *Wine Enthusiast Magazine* named Turback's "one of the wine-friendliest restaurants in America" and the restaurant's daring all-local lineup was awarded "Best American Wine List" by *Restaurant Business Magazine.*

Over the years, Michael has served as judge in numerous wine competitions and lectured on wine at Cornell University (his Alma Mater).

Besides an extraordinary appreciation of regional food and wine, he is well-informed and patriotically enthusiastic about all things Finger Lakes, and he knows the region inside and out.

In a review of Michael's 2005 well-researched book, *Greetings from the Finger Lakes: A Food and Wine Lover's Companion*, Kevin Zraly, founder of the Windows on the World Wine School, wrote: "Michael Turback has captured the region's personality with his own passion for food and wine."

More recently, in cooperation with Culinart Media, Michael developed the region's first and most comprehensive culinary travel app, *Tour the Finger Lakes*.

Introduction

"Adventure is just bad planning."
— Roald Amundsen, Polar Explorer

Wine can be a lot of things, but it starts with pleasure. The Finger Lakes region offers plenty of pleasures, and this book will help you get right to them. Nearly ten years ago, I sipped and tasted my way around the region for *Greeting from the Finger Lakes: A Food and Wine Lovers Companion*, and — yadda, yadda, yadda — here I am doing it again.

Whether visitor or native, I'm going to assume that your time is valuable, so in this more practical, user-friendly format I've decided to show you how to make the most of a day trip or long weekend with the kind of fresh and knowing information that could only come from the familiarity of someone who eats, sips, and breathes this place. I'll see to it that your pilgrimage to this ascending wine country destination is less a freelance "adventure" and more an efficient, rewarding experience.

True to the topic, this book covers a lot of ground, both enologically and geographically. While the sprawl can seem daunting, I'll help you navigate around the long, non-traversable lakes, avoid random tastings of the "usual suspects," focus squarely on the good stuff, and make the most of your schedule. I'll suggest the best places to stay (avoiding accommodations that resemble the Bates Motel), and since there is a natural affinity between vineyard and kitchen in our region, I'll introduce both local favorites and newcomers to the restaurant scene.

Film buffs will remember that in *The Graduate*, the "one word" of advice Mr. McGuire offers to Benjamin is "plastics." If there is an essential, singular word to offer on the matter of Finger Lakes wines, I suggest that word is "Riesling," and I urge you to pay special attention to this joyous varietal on any visit. The region has adopted a focused approach centered on Riesling as its lead grape.

It may never be quite what you expect, which is exactly why you should start acquainting yourself with this often misunderstood wine, beloved by chefs and sommeliers for its food friendliness. First, lose the notion that this is just a sweet wine. Stylistically versatile and easy drinking, Riesling has the uncanny ability to run the gamut of styles and flavors — from candy-sweet to bone-dry, with aromas of citrus, stone fruit, honeysuckle or petrol. At each place on the spectrum, you find a wine of different character, filling different needs and offering different pleasures. It is said that Riesling represents the purest form of winemaking — there is no oak, no malolactic fermentation, no blending with other grapes to promote complexity or hide winemaking mistakes.

Many of our region's Rieslings are unquestionably as wonderfully expressive as the revered German and Alsatian counterparts in their Old World home, and as the most widely-planted European-descended Vinifera grape, you will encounter exceptional bottles throughout wine country — most selling below twenty dollars. There's an erupting wellspring of euphoria about our region's success with this varietal. We're still giddy about a profile in *La Vigne*, the French wine industry magazine, calling the Finger Lakes "the New Riesling Kingdom."

Besides the celebrated Rieslings, you will find a truly unexpected variety of limited production, intellectually stimulating wines as you sip your way around the lakes. From humble, quaffable versions to vibrant, award-winning entries in state, national, and international competitions, the choices are almost embarrassingly rich. Many bottles not only offer pleasures simply because they are delicious, they also have something to say about where they came from and the people who made them. Informed tastings provide the chance to stretch your boundaries, to try something new, something different.

There is a saying around these parts that it takes a lot of good beer to make good wine — for many local winemakers there's only one thing that hits the spot at the end of the day and that's a heady, hoppy brew. So where there's wine, there's beer, and as growers revive the region's hop farms, microbreweries have emerged among the vines. We're beginning to approach the craft with the exaltation once relegated to wine, to see beer as more than just a beverage designed for quenching thirst and delivering a buzz. Brewery and brewpub-crawls have become part of local culture.

When *Thrillist* assembled a panel of esteemed wine experts and sommeliers to pick the best wine regions in the United States, the Finger Lakes topped the list (ahead of Willamette Valley, Oregon and both Napa and Sonoma in California).

Carole King crooned that life is a tapestry, and that's certainly true for the Finger Lakes of New York. Consider the book you hold in your hands as my personal invitation to the amazing tapestry of the region. Read on, my friends, as you begin your journey to this remarkable place.

Michael Turback
www.michaelturback.com

Overview

The Finger Lakes region of New York State encompasses more than 9,000 square miles and 14 counties, bordered on the north from Syracuse to Rochester and nearly as far south as the Pennsylvania border — that's roughly the size of New Hampshire or Vermont, and slightly larger than the state of New Jersey. The major Finger Lakes, from east to west are: Skaneateles, Cayuga, Seneca, Keuka, and Canandaigua. Cities and villages, including Skaneateles, Ithaca, Geneva, Watkins Glen, Penn Yan, Hammondsport and Canandaigua, are located at head or foot of lakes that reminded early map-makers of the fingers of a hand.

For all the decidedly contemporary people and places you'll find here, visiting the Finger Lakes inevitably involves interacting with history.

During the ancient Ice Age, up to a mile-high mass of ice plowed into this terrain from the north like a giant bulldozer, carving deep canyons into the bedrock and depositing a shallow layer of topsoil on sloping shale beds. As the glaciers retreated, melting ice sheets filled deep claw marks to form a series of parallel lakes, surrounded by copious deposits of rocky soils and characterized by a wide-ranging variety of microclimates.

The earliest immigrants understood that the agricultural abundance of this land was a precious gift. Enabled by the moderating effects of the deep, narrow bodies of water, they were able to harvest bumper crops of produce — including grapes — not otherwise expected to prosper this far north. In winter, the lakes almost never freeze, moderating harsh cold to protect the dormant vines, while in summer they air-condition the vineyards.

Hammondsport, at the southern end of Keuka Lake, was the site of both the birth and the re-birth of the wine industry here. In 1855, the cultivation of grapes attracted an enterprising Frenchman by the name of Charles D. Champlin, and by 1860 he had become the principal organizer of the Pleasant Valley Wine Company, producing bottle-fermented sparkling wines from hillside-grown Catawba grapes. Then, almost exactly 100 years after Champlin first persisted with the grapey native wines, an eccentric Ukranian-born professor of plant science challenged prevailing wisdom by cultivating classic European grapes in his Hammondsport vineyard.

With the experience he gained coping with the extreme winters of his homeland, Konstantin Frank produced remarkable wines from Vinifera grapes planted on a thermally-stable slope of Keuka Lake. He developed his own rootstock mother blocks and tinkered with various clones, successfully igniting a movement that dramatically changed the course of winegrowing in the cool climate. Of the varieties he pioneered, Riesling has become the signature wine of the Finger Lakes, its quality comparable to classic German wines of the Mosel and Germanic-influenced wines of the French Alsace. Dr. Frank's contribution to winemaking has reached well beyond his years.

Closely intertwined with the success of new wines in the Finger Lakes is the recognition of something called terroir, the mysterious French term that encapsulates the geology and microclimate of a particular place, but it means much more than that. It speaks to the human hands that grow the grapes, how the soil and the lakes are unmistakably expressed in the harvest, and how the disparate components of locale account for wines that reflect their origin.

The massive amounts of water in the deep lakes temper the extremes of Upstate New York weather, lengthening the growing season and making it possible for lakeside grapes to ripen sufficiently to develop intense fruit concentrations. Intricacies of the soils, deposited by the glaciers, also have a profound impact on the flavors of the wines. The abundant deposits of primeval Devonian shale produce wines with steely minerality, natural acidity, liveliness and balanced alcohol. Shale allows Riesling in particular to express its terroir, as evidenced by the mineral components found in drier styles, and part of Riesling's ascent in the Finger Lakes can be credited to the very climate and characteristics that other grapes find so challenging.

Thanks to the confluence of circumstances — habitable climate, the earth in which the grapes are grown, and a new generation of winemaking talent — the Finger Lakes region has become home to some of the most exciting wines made today.

Tasting Etiquette

You will find tasting rooms stitched together along rural country roads, mostly hugging the lakes. The spaces are as wildly different as the local wines themselves, from large, sometimes lavish rooms to folding tables among the barrels. Tasting rooms provide sample tastings, poured by trained staffs whose primary concern is your education and enjoyment of their products. At a few stops you will meet some of our most important winemakers.

Before heading out, there are a few practical details and important reminders you will need to help make the most of your visit.

Many tasting rooms are open year-round, typically seven days a week. Peak tourist season begins in June and runs through October, and in the off-season, expect shorter hours, mainly on weekends, or by appointment only. (The best time to tour wine country is when it is clothed with the verdure of midsummer). Wine tastings are usually not available on holidays such as Easter, Thanksgiving, and Christmas, and New Year's Day. The more popular wineries can be crowded, especially during the tourist season, which means less attention paid to you. You might consider a weekday visit if it fits your schedule. Crowds diminish substantially and pourers have more time to talk shop.

Call in advance if your group will be larger than five. Some of the smaller wineries don't have space for buses or limousines. Others like to know in advance if large groups will be arriving so they can provide enough staff. Always make an appointment where indicated — if the winery sign reads "By Appointment Only," don't pop in unannounced. Most of the time all it takes is a quick phone call to arrange a visit. Be prepared to show a valid form of I.D.

A successful tasting room experience begins with preparation. Start the day with a good breakfast and continue to snack throughout the day. Make sure you're hydrated before leaving home. Drinking water between each tasting will have little benefit if you're starting out with an empty (water) tank. Pack plenty of bottled water for your trip and drink often. Take along a large cooler. If you buy wines on your trip, you'll need a place to store them during the day. Tossing them in a hot trunk may "cook" them before you get them home.

Proper tasting requires the ability to experience the aroma or bouquet of the wines. Wearing perfume, cologne, after-shave, sun tan lotion, or even chapstick or lipstick can interfere with your full appreciation of the aromatics, and with that of other visitors in the tasting room. Minimize the use of anything that might have a distracting scent. No chewing gum or smoking. And skip the coffee. One cup will kill your palate for a good half hour.

There is no cost for admission to tasting rooms, although most wineries require a fee to taste the offerings. When a fee is charged, it's okay for two people to share the same glass and pay only one tasting fee. Tasting fees will sometimes be deducted from the price of bottle purchases, and a few wineries will include a souvenir glass with the fee.

Don't crowd the tasting counter. If you arrive at a busy tasting bar, await your turn, then back away from the bar after receiving your next tasting to give others a chance to progress in their tasting order.

Keep your cell phone on vibrate. Step outside if it is necessary to use your phone so as not to disturb others.

Most wineries will have a detailed list of wines they'd like you to try. But keep in mind, you do not have to taste every wine on the list, in fact, it often makes more sense to ignore a winery's full offering, focus on a particular varietal, or cherry-pick as few as one or two wines per stop. You may, for instance, decide to taste only Riesling and Cabernet Franc, sampling just those at each winery. This technique can help you learn how different vineyards, different vintages, and different winemakers affect the finished wine.

Recommendations throughout this book will help to identify specific proficiencies and best bottles without being overwhelmed. Visiting a winery knowing exactly what you want to taste identifies you as a more confident and better educated consumer. You will likely receive special attention and have the standard tasting fee waived.

Keep in mind that you are in a tasting room, not a bar. Only a small amount of wine — usually an ounce — will be poured into your glass. Correct wine etiquette does not dictate that you must finish every tasting portion. Taste buds wear out easily.

The most basic rule is to drink white wine before red, and always dry before sweet. Be sure to save late harvest and dessert wines for last. Wine sampling is about finding the flavors that you enjoy the most, and you are never wrong when it comes to choosing wines that you enjoy. Taste each wine carefully and savor each sip.

If a winery provides tasting notes, read as you taste and see if you recognize any of the aromas or flavors listed in the notes. (Descriptors at the back of this book will help you put words to the aromas and flavors you're tasting). Bring your own notebook and keep track of what you like about each wine. Taking notes not only helps you to remember what you tasted, but it's a signal to attentive pourers that you are serious about the tasting exercise. This will often get you a bit more personalized treatment.

Most tasting rooms provide crackers or other neutral food to clear the palate after sampling each particular wine. Feel free to bring your own (I carry a box of Carr's Table Water Biscuits), or start your wine-tasting day by picking up a baguette at one of the local bakeries and take it along as your portable palate cleanser.

Rinsing your glass is a good idea when the tasting moves from whites to reds or to dessert wines. Some wineries discourage rinsing with water as it can affect the next wine and they'll insist on rinsing it for you with little wine.

The sense of smell is one of the most sophisticated of all the senses. In order to experience the true bouquet of a wine, begin by swirling. To properly swirl, place the glass flat on the table, hold it by the stem, and rotate it in a circle to aerate the wine. Then stick your nose right in there — it's been suggested that a sense of smell may be more than ten thousand times more sensitive than that of taste. To skip the aroma or bouquet of a wine is to deprive yourself of an important part of the pleasure. (Don't swirl sparkling wines; bubbles already provide proper aeration).

Once in your mouth, roll the wine around so that it coats the front, back, and side of your tongue. Slowly savoring a small amount of each wine you sample not only helps maintain sobriety, it also helps you fully appreciate each wine. Drinking water between sips helps in this regard. Use the spit bucket. That's what it's there for. Use it even if you have a designated driver. Don't be afraid to dump any remainder of wine once you've tasted it, your pourer will not be offended and will recognize your empty glass as a signal to pour the next taste. In crowded tasting rooms, or where buckets are too full for comfort, request a paper or plastic cup for more discreet spitting.

Under ordinary circumstances, asking for a second taste of one particular wine is inappropriate. However, if you're sincerely interested in buying the wine, let the pourer know your intentions.

You are under no obligation to buy wine at the tasting room. However, if you fall in love with a wine, by all means buy it at the winery. Many winery tasting rooms are pouring wines not available elsewhere. Smaller production wineries have limited distribution, and their wines can be difficult (or impossible) to find in a wine shop or liquor store. You can typically buy by the bottle or by the case (12 bottles). Wineries will often apply a case discount (and sometimes a half-case discount), mixed or matched.

Unfortunately, some producers are pressured to price their wines at a certain level, lest they not be taken seriously. Don't judge a wine by its price.

I applaud the increasing use of screw caps, replacing traditional or synthetic corks even if they do not allow the romance of removing the cork. Oxygen has a deleterious effect on wine, and screw tops are close to airtight.

The time spent in a tasting room or winery is a time for discovery and learning. Ask questions. Most tasting room personnel are very knowledgeable about the wine, winery and vineyards. Their explanations, descriptions, and stories can add to your appreciation of their wines. Tipping is not routine and not expected. A few of the larger wineries provide tours. If a tour is available, by all means participate.

No one under the age of 21 may sample wine. Since they won't be allowed to taste wines, young children may find the tasting-room experience tedious. For this reason, some wineries discourage (but usually don't prohibit) kids. If you plan to bring your kids along on a trip to wine country, have planned activities for them while you are tasting. They can become easily bored. Keep them away from breakable objects in the tasting room.

One more thing. While you will be rewarded with many very good red wines in the region, your more exceptional finds will likely be whites. A common misconception is that red wines are more serious than white wines. Once you've sipped a Finger Lakes Riesling, you will discover that red wines are no more worthy of veneration over white wines than red cars over white cars.

Most of the above applies to beer tastings as well as wine tastings, with one exception. Some of the flavors and aromas in beer are picked up on the back of the palate and in the throat. To fully experience the flavor of beer, one must swallow it. Practical and responsible tastings require only a sip or two of each beer, not the full pour, and drink plenty of water throughout the day to stay hydrated. Don't forget to bring along a cooler on your beer trek to safely transport growlers.

How to Use This Book

Finding, trying and retaining information about new wines or craft beers can be overwhelming for even the most ardent traveler, let alone planning for meals along the way and finding comforting accommodations at the end of the day.

I have set out to provide a practical resource for anyone making a trip to the region, removing the intimidation factor that often surrounds its geographic scale. Within the limitations of a day trip or a weekend visit, I've carefully plotted a range of driving tours, selecting high points from a well-informed insider's view and making it possible to follow from one place to the next in a reasonably allotted time. Travelers who have more days to spend may want to supplement this guide with more comprehensive information available from winery and brewery Internet sites. Or, since the format of this book carves up the region into sections, itineraries could easily be strung together to make up a longer trip. (Beware of the free "Wine Trail" and "Beer Trail" brochures widely distributed around the lakes; these guides only include dues-paying members and omit some of the must-visit wineries and microbreweries).

The book's structure is divided into three separate sections, each based on primary interest or agenda. This is, after all, wine country, so you'll find winery stops on all itineraries.

If your intention is to focus mostly on wines, go directly to Section 1. Other sections allow you to diversify visits or expand subsequent visits with stops at microbreweries and brewpubs (Section 2), or encourage you to explore the natural beauty, architectural wonders, and historic sites of the region (Section 3).

While New York's Finger Lakes may seem like halfway to nowhere, locals will remind you that our region sits within 300 miles of 30 percent of the entire U.S. population. If you think of the territory as a giant rectangle, almost any traveler will enter through a city, town, or village — a portal at each of the four corners.

Travelers from New York City, the New York-New Jersey-Connecticut metropolitan area, Philadelphia and all points South-East enter through Ithaca.

From Syracuse, Albany, Montreal, Boston, New England and all points North-East, travelers enter through Skaneateles.

From Rochester, Buffalo, Niagara Falls, Toronto, and all points North-West, travelers enter through Canandaigua.

If arriving from Pittsburgh, Cleveland, Indianapolis, Chicago, and other points South-West, travelers enter through Hammondsport.

To begin, choose the section that represents your primary interest. Then, depending on your point of entry, select the length of your visit. Your schedule need not be set in stone. The best experiences include "must-visits" mixed in with some flexibility, and some will prefer to travel at their own pace and take their own detours. Permission granted.

As you cruise around the rural lakeside roads, drive carefully. Don't overindulge, and don't drive if you've overindulged. If you can, bring a designated driver; if not, always spit when you taste.

Please Note: From early Spring through late Fall, most wineries will be open to the public throughout the day (usually from 10 AM to 5 PM). During the off-season, days and hours of operation vary greatly from winery to winery, and brewery hours can be even more unpredictable, so phone ahead to inquire about tasting opportunities. Of course, always call ahead for dinner reservations and plan in advance for overnight accommodations.

Section 1: Wine Trails: Wineries

Section 2: Beer Trails: Breweries and Brewpubs

Section 3: Scenic and Historic Points of Interest

Entry Point:

CANANDAIGUA

(NORTH - WEST)

WINE TRAILS

DAY TRIP

LAFAYETTE RESTAURANT ✪

408 Lakeshore Drive, Canandaigua, NY 14424
Phone: (585) 394-5383
Online: www.lafayettemotelandrestaurant.com

Breakfast at this 50-year-old local institution is a special pleasure. In a homey, diner-style setting, plates are piled high with eggs, waffles, pancakes, French toast, homemade breads, cinnamon buns, and fat pies. The staff is friendly and service is usually pretty quick. Take home a bag of house-blend coffee beans.

>Take Lakeshore Drive to East Lake Road, turn right onto Routes 5&20 heading east to Geneva (about 20 minutes), then follow Route 14 South along the western shore of Seneca Lake.

FOX RUN VINEYARDS ♟

670 Route 14, Penn Yan, NY 14527
Phone: (800) 636-9786
Online: www.foxrunvineyards.com

At first sniff and sip, you will know you are onto something good here. For more than a century Fox Run was a dairy farm. The first grapes were planted in 1984, and the barn, erected shortly after the Civil War, was restored and opened as a winery in 1990 by Larry and Adele Wildrick. Three years later it was sold to Scott Osborn and investor Andy Hale, drawn to the property for its promise of fine winegrowing. With 60 acres of vines in production, Fox Run is one of the region's most influential enterprises, a testament to the ability of winemaker Peter Bell whose Rieslings are among the region's best. Don't miss Peter's Devonian Red, a blend of Cab Franc, Lemberger, and Merlot. In 2008, Fox Run was chosen as one of the top 100 wineries in the world by *Wine and Spirits Magazine.*

RED TAIL RIDGE WINERY ♟

846 Route 14, Penn Yan, NY 14527
Phone: (315) 536-4580
Online: www.redtailridgewinery.com

After creating a name for herself as Vice President of Viticulture and

Enology R&D at Gallo, the world's largest winery, Nancy Irelan headed east to establish Red Tail Ridge in 2004. Working with her husband, Mike Schnelle, who manages the wisely-planted vineyards, Nancy's focus is Riesling, crafting in styles from dry to late harvest (made from grapes afflicted with the "noble rot" of botrytized bunches), including a "spontaneously fermented" Riesling. The "Obscure Red Varietal Series," small productions of Blaufrankisch, Dornfelder, and Teroldego, offer a contrast to much of the region. Red Tail Ridge's modest tasting room doesn't hint at the outstanding wines they produce.

HERMANN J. WIEMER VINEYARD

3962 Route 14, Dundee, NY 14837
Phone: (800) 371- 7971
Online: www.wiemer.com

If Riesling were a religion, Hermann Wiemer would be a high priest. He is a native of Germany, descended from a long line of winemakers in a Riesling-producing region, so it was quite natural that he made his reputation with prize-winning wines from Germany's "noble grape," meticulous about growing, picking, and winemaking. Fred Merwarth faithfully maintains the legacy and heritage of Mr. Wiemer, who established the Finger Lakes as one of the premier Riesling terroirs in the world. This treasure of a spot has been consistently recognized as one of the world's Top 100 Estates by *Wine & Spirits Magazine*. Taste the single-vineyard Rieslings side-by-side to compare and contrast unique characters.

GLENORA WINE CELLARS

5435 Route 14, Dundee, NY 14837
Phone: (607) 243-5511
Online: www.glenora.com

This is one of the few wineries that has it all. Glenora was the brainchild of three eminent grapegrowers, led by Gene Pierce, a Cornell Aggie. In 1977, when passage of the Farm Winery Act handed grape growers incentives to become vintners, Gene and his pals Ed Dalrymple and Eastman Beers, relying on fruit from their own vineyards, got started in the wine business. Towering above Seneca Lake and carpeted in meticulous vineyards, Glenora, a key player in the revival of the Finger Lakes as a wine-growing region, produces good-to-terrific, humanely-priced wines. A credentialed technician by the name of Steve DiFrancisco is responsible for the range of offerings here, most notably Dry Riesling, arguably the best bargains in the region.

VERAISONS

5435 Route 14, Dundee, NY 14837
Phone: (607) 243-5511
Online: www.glenora.com/Restaurant/Veraisons-Restaurant
Corkage Fee: none for Glenora wines; $10 for other wines

Its name the viticultural term for the onset of ripening of wine grapes, Veraisons is part of the Glenora winery complex, a handsome dining room overlooking estate vineyards and Seneca Lake. Weather permitting, ask for a table on the outdoor terrace to soak up wine country in all its glory.

>Reverse course on Route 14 heading north to Geneva.

ANTHONY ROAD WINE COMPANY

1020 Anthony Road (off Route 14), Penn Yan, NY 14527
Phone: (800) 559-2182
Online: www.anthonyroadwine.com

In 1973, John and Ann Martini settled on 100 acres of farmland where they planted grapes to sell to the giant Taylor Wine Company. By the late 1980s they formalized the Anthony Road Wine Company, and the venture's first bottle of wine was released in 1990. The winery's excellence is best expressed in Rieslings fermented without the addition of cultured yeast. Winemaker Peter Becraft produces dry, semi-dry and semi-sweet Riesling, as well as an extraordinary Riesling Trockenbeeren.

BILLSBORO WINERY

4760 Route 14, Geneva, NY 14456
Phone: (315) 789-9538
Online: www.billsborowinery.com

The winery was started as a retirement project by Dr. Robert Pool, es teemed professor of viticulture at Cornell's New York State Agricultural Experiment Station in Geneva. With his passing, the estate was purchased by winemaker Vinny Aliperti, who apprenticed at Wölffer Estate on Long Island under Roman Roth, then in the Finger Lakes at Hermann J. Wiemer Vineyard, where he was first exposed to Riesling production. In 2001 he joined Atwater Estate Vineyards, where he continues to make wine. Vinny is among the handful of Finger Lakes winemakers who source grapes from select blocks in the Hazlitt family's Sawmill Creek Vineyard, for exceptional Rieslings, both dry and semi-dry. (Tastings include a wine & chocolate pairing).

>*Continue on Route 14 heading north to Routes 5&20 West, turn left onto Pre-Emption Road, and drive one mile.*

RAVINES WINE CELLARS

400 Barracks Road (off Pre-Emption Road), Geneva, NY 14456
Phone: (315) 781-7007
Online: www.ravineswinecellars.com

French wine lovers worship the land, but in the Finger Lakes, the winemaker is king. Morten Hallgren was raised among the casks and vines of his family's winemaking estate in Provence, so the French influence is strong here, both in the wines and the winery. You might say that Morten is to the Riesling grape what Yo-Yo Ma is to the cello. For his exquisite, Alsace-inspired Rieslings, he purchases a spectrum of grapes from a range of sites, convincing growers to lower croploads for more concentrated, complex wines. Grapes are whole bunch pressed to ensure gentle extraction of flavor compounds, retaining delicate fruit characters, floral and mineral elements. Deposits of residual yeast are stirred at the end of fermentation, a technique the French refer to as battonage, to soften acidity. A converted 100-year-old barn houses the tasting room, adjacent to a state-of-the-art winemaking facility. Ravines was recently named by *Wine Spectator* among the 100 best wineries in the world. (Wine tastings include chocolate and cheese pairings).

>*Follow Pre-Emption Road back to Routes 5&20 heading west to Canandaigua (about 20 minutes). Turn left onto South Main Street.*

NEW YORK WINE & CULINARY CENTER

800 South Main Street, Canandaigua, NY 14424
Phone: (585) 394-7070
Online: www.nywcc.com

A faithful adherence to the bounty of New York wine, craft beer, food and agriculture draws crowds to this tasting room, culinary demonstration theater, hands-on kitchen, gift boutique, outdoor garden and Upstairs Bistro whose menu showcases New York State ingredients. Score a table on the deck and enjoy Caesar salads, grilled pizzas, sandwiches, and main dishes overlooking Canandaigua Lake. New York State wines by the bottle, glass, or flight. After dinner, head over to Kershaw Park and stroll along the lakefront walkway before calling it a night.

THE INN ON THE LAKE

770 South Main Street, Canandaigua, NY 14424
Phone: (800) 228-2801
Online: www.theinnonthelake.com

Perched at the edge of Canandaigua Lake's north shore, just a few steps from the Wine & Culinary Center. Request a room with lakefront patio or balcony, and bring a bathing suit for the indoor or outdoor pool. Good selection of local wines at either The Lounge or The Sand Bar, the seasonal poolside bar.

Entry Point:

CANANDAIGUA

(NORTH - WEST)

WINE TRAILS

WEEKEND TOUR

Friday

RHEINBLICK GERMAN RESTAURANT

224 S. Main Street, Canandaigua, NY 14424
Phone: (585) 905-0950
Online: www.rheinblick.hostei.com
Corkage Fee: none

The first wave of German immigrants arrived in Western New York in the mid-1800s, growing hops and honing beer brewing to a fine art. Dinner in the cozy dining room or at a table in the adjacent alley includes an impressive selection of German beers, both draft and bottled, to accompany schnitzels, wursts, bratens, and other pork, veal, and chicken entrées, along with starters and traditional sides like sauerkraut, egg noodles, and spätzle. Dr. Konstantin Frank Grüner Veltliner and Merlot supplement the list of German wines.

THE INN ON THE LAKE

770 South Main Street, Canandaigua, NY 14424
Phone: (800) 228-2801
Online: www.theinnonthelake.com

Perched at the edge of Canandaigua Lake's north shore, just a few steps from the Wine & Culinary Center. Request a room with lakefront patio or balcony, and bring a bathing suit for the indoor or outdoor pool. Good selection of local wines at either The Lounge or The Sand Bar, the seasonal poolside bar.

Saturday

LAFAYETTE RESTAURANT

408 Lakeshore Drive, Canandaigua, NY 14424
Phone: (585) 394-5383
Online: www.lafayettemotelandrestaurant.com

Breakfast at this 50-year-old local institution is a special pleasure. In a

homey, diner-style setting, plates are piled high with eggs, waffles, pancakes, French toast, homemade breads, cinnamon buns, and fat pies.
The staff is friendly and service is usually pretty quick. Take home a
bag of house-blend coffee beans.

>*Drive west on Lakeshore Drive. Park along the lakefront near the Culi-
nary Center.*

KERSHAW PARK

A bedroom community for nearby Rochester and historically a popular
summer retreat for wealthy city folk (Humphrey Bogart's family maintained a summertime cottage on the lake), Canandaigua was built on
the site of a Seneca Indian village, becoming an important railroad
junction and home port for several steamboats by the mid-19th century.
Between 1920 and 1936, old cars among other things were dumped in
the lake here to anchor the earth and rocks used to make the park.
Stroll along the lakefront walkways or have an impromptu picnic at
Kershaw Park, just off Lakeshore Drive, the original shoreline of the
lake.

NEW YORK WINE & CULINARY CENTER

800 South Main Street, Canandaigua, NY 14424
Phone: (585) 394-7070
Online: www.nywcc.com

Keep walking. Now you're headed to the New York Wine & Culinary
Center, northwest gateway to the bounty of food and wine produced
throughout the state. The Center includes a culinary demonstration
theater, hands-on kitchen, bistro, gift boutique, and tasting room where
you can acquaint yourself with wines and beers from around the state.

**Drive to Routes 5&20 heading east to Geneva (about 20 minutes). Turn
onto Route 14 heading south, along the western shore of Seneca Lake.*

FOX RUN VINEYARDS

670 Route 14, Penn Yan, NY 14527
Phone: (800) 636-9786

Online: www.foxrunvineyards.com

At first sniff and sip, you will know you are onto something good here. For more than a century Fox Run was a dairy farm. The first grapes were planted in 1984, and the barn, erected shortly after the Civil War, was restored and opened as a winery in 1990 by Larry and Adele Wildrick. Three years later it was sold to Scott Osborn and investor Andy Hale, drawn to the property for its promise of fine winegrowing. With 60 acres of vines in production, Fox Run is one of the region's most influential enterprises, a testament to the ability of winemaker Peter Bell whose Rieslings are among the region's best. Don't miss Peter's Devonian Red, a blend of Cab Franc, Lemberger, and Merlot (named for a chapter in the region's geological history). In 2008, Fox Run was chosen as one of the top 100 wineries in the world by *Wine and Spirits Magazine.*

RED TAIL RIDGE WINERY

846 Route 14, Penn Yan, NY 14527
Phone: (315) 536-4580
Online: www.redtailridgewinery.com

After creating a name for herself as Vice President of Viticulture and Enology R&D at Gallo, the world's largest winery, Nancy Irelan headed east to establish Red Tail Ridge in 2004. Working with her husband, Mike Schnelle, who manages the wisely-planted vineyards, Nancy's focus is Riesling, crafting in styles from dry to late harvest (made from grapes afflicted with the "noble rot" of botrytized bunches), including a "spontaneously fermented" Riesling. The "Obscure Red Varietal Series," small productions of Blaufrankisch, Dornfelder, and Teroldego, offer a contrast to much of the region. Red Tail Ridge's modest tasting room doesn't hint at the outstanding wines they produce.

ANTHONY ROAD WINE COMPANY

1020 Anthony Road, Penn Yan, NY 14527
Phone: (800) 559-2182
Online: www.anthonyroadwine.com

In 1973, John and Ann Martini settled on 100 acres of farmland where they planted grapes to sell to the giant Taylor Wine Company. By the late 1980s they formalized the Anthony Road Wine Company, and the venture's first bottle of wine was released in 1990. The winery's excellence is best expressed in Rieslings fermented without the addition of cultured yeast. Winemaker Peter Becraft produces dry, semi-dry and semi-sweet Riesling, as well as an extraordinary Riesling Trockenbeeren.

HERMANN J. WIEMER VINEYARD

3962 Route 14, Dundee, NY 14837
Phone: (800) 371-7971
Online: www.wiemer.com

If Riesling were a religion, Hermann Wiemer would be a high priest. He is a native of Germany, descended from a long line of winemakers in a Riesling-producing region, so it was quite natural that he made his reputation with prize-winning wines from Germany's "noble grape." He was meticulous about growing, picking, and winemaking. Fred Merwarth faithfully maintains the legacy and heritage of Mr. Wiemer, who established the Finger Lakes as one of the premier Riesling terroirs in the world. This treasure of a spot has been consistently recognized as one of the world's Top 100 Estates by *Wine & Spirits Magazine*. Taste the single-vineyard Rieslings side-by-side to compare and contrast unique characters.

FLX WIENERY

5090 Route 14, Dundee, NY 14838
Phone: (607) 243-7100
Online: www.flxwienery.com
Corkage Fee: none

The idea of getting a decent "wiener" while on the hoof along the wine trail is the brainstorm of Christopher Bates, a kind of culinary James Franco — he's a Master Sommelier (one of only 200 or so people worldwide), winemaker (Element Winery), cheesemaker, and chef (formerly of Hotel Fauchère in Milford, Pennsylvania). Step up to the counter for Shirk's Smoked Dogs or Zweigle's White Hots, served single or double with creative topping combos and irresistible sides. Sip shakes, floats, egg creams, or bring-your-own local wine and drink from Riedel crystal (for a small fee).

GLENORA WINE CELLARS

5435 Route 14, Dundee, NY 14837
Phone: (607) 243-5511
Online: www.glenora.com

This is one of the few wineries that has it all. Glenora was the brainchild of three eminent grapegrowers, led by Gene Pierce, a Cornell Aggie. In 1977, when passage of the Farm Winery Act handed grape growers incentives to become vintners, Gene and his pals Ed Dalrymple and Eastman Beers, relying on fruit from their own vineyards, got started in the wine business. Towering above Seneca Lake and carpeted by meticulous vineyards, Glenora, a key player in the revival of the Finger Lakes as a wine-growing region, produces good-to-terrific, humanely-priced wines. A credentialed technician by the name of Steve DiFrancisco is responsible for the range of offerings here, most notably Dry Riesling, arguably the best bargains in the region.

FULKERSON WINERY

5576 Route 14, Dundee, NY 14837
Phone: (607) 243-7883
Online: www.fulkersonwinery.com

Steeped in history, the Fulkerson farm is comprised of vineyards, pastures, and ancient oak trees on rolling land that has been in the hearts and hands of the same family for two hundred years. The property was purchased in 1805 by Caleb Fulkerson, a veteran of the Revolutionary War, passed down to Samuel, then to Harlan, Harlan Jr., Roger, and now to Sayre Fulkerson, the sixth generation owner, who is charged with preservation of the family farm as an agricultural enterprise. Nearly half the juice pressed here is sold to amateur winemakers. The remainder is crafted into a range of varietals, including such oddities as Dornfelder, Vincent, and Diamond. Pay special attention to the "William Vigne" Rieslings (named after the first of the Fulkersons in the New World).

MAGNUS RIDGE VINEYARD AND WINERY

6148 Route 14, Rock Stream NY 14878
Phone: (607) 243-3611
Online: www.magnusridge.com

It would be hard to find two people who better symbolize the region's future than Matt and Sandy Downey, engineers by profession, who have erected a movie-set version of a European country winery, housing a "mongo-sized" tasting room, gift shop, and café, surrounded by ponds, walking trails, and waterfalls. Estate-grown (at off-site vineyards) Chardonnay, Pinot Gris, and Gewurztraminer are eclipsed by a pleasurable, uncomplicated, semi-dry Riesling.

LAKEWOOD VINEYARDS

4024 Route 14, Watkins Glen, NY 14891
Phone: (607) 535-9252
Online: www.lakewoodvineyards.com

In April of 1951, Frank Stamp packed his wife and their three kids into the family Hudson and drove from Maryland to the patch of lakeside property he had purchased with his life savings. Within a year they had planted five acres of grapes in the fertile soil, and the Stamps have been faithful stewards of these vineyards ever since. Chris, first-born of the third generation, earned a food science degree from Cornell, then served as winemaker at Plane's Cayuga Vineyard before joining the family enterprise. His craft shines through in the Lakewood catalog of vinifera, hybrid, labrusca, ice wines, fortified wines, and honey mead. Part of the secret of the Lakewood success is the family vineyard, of course. Rieslings are blended from grapes grown on five specialized blocks. Each specific location is chosen according to the depth, structure, and composition of the soil in order to achieve optimum expressions, the final brushstrokes for his masterpieces.

>*Continue on Route 14 heading south to the village of Watkins Glen.*

WATKINS GLEN STATE PARK

Work up an appetite at the most famous of Finger Lakes parks, with a reputation for leaving visitors spellbound. The glen's stream descends 400 feet past 200-foot cliffs, generating 19 waterfalls along its course. In 1933 President Franklin Roosevelt created the Civilian Conservation Corps in an effort to put unemployed men to work. They were responsible for building many of the present day pathways winding over and under waterfalls and through the spray of Cavern Cascade. It's a 3-mile round trip if you do the whole thing; wear comfortable shoes.

GRAFT WINE & CIDER BAR

204 North Franklin Street (Route 14), Watkins Glen, NY 14891
Phone: (607) 210-4324
Online: www.facebook.com

Its name refers to the process of placing a shoot system of one grapevine species on the rootstock of another, not to political corruption in Albany. Sip local wines and ciders at the convivial bar, lined with a well of polished lake stones, or in one of the comfy benches; feast on creative, thoughtfully-prepared small plates, designed to share and pair by well-known local chefs Christina and Jonah McKeough.

WATKINS GLEN HARBOR HOTEL

16 North Franklin Street (Route 14), Watkins Glen, NY 14891
Phone: (607) 535-6116
Online: www.watkinsglenharborhotel.com

Nesting on the Southern-most point of Seneca Lake, hotel guestrooms are appointed with comfy pillow-topped mattresses covered with 310-thread count linens, plush duvet covers and feather pillows. Request a room with a view of the lake and enjoy a glass of local wine on your balcony.

Sunday

BLUE POINTE GRILLE

16 North Franklin Street (Route 14), Watkins Glen, NY 14891
Phone: (607) 535-6116
Online: www.watkinsglenharborhotel.com
Breakfast Hours: 7 AM to 11 AM

Start off your day with above-average hotel dining room breakfast fare, including omelets, made-to-order eggs, steak & eggs, cereals, waffles, French toast, pancakes, and coffee or espresso. Ask for a table on the lakeside patio and enjoy breakfast al fresco overlooking Seneca harbor.

>*Beginning at the corner North Franklin Street (Route 14) and 4th Street (Route 414), follow Route 414 north along the eastern shore of Seneca Lake.*

FINGER LAKES DISTILLING

4676 Route 414, Burdett, NY 14818
Phone: (607) 546-5510
Online: www.fingerlakesdistilling.com

The striking micro-distillery stands high above Seneca Lake, housing a custom-built 300-gallon, German-made Holstein pot still for the small-batch distillation of local grapes, including Gewürztraminer, Muscat and Catawba. Among the impressive elixirs is Seneca Drums, a London dry-style gin, energized with eleven botanicals, and McKenzie Rye Whiskey, distilled from New York-grown grain, aged in charred casks and finished in sherry barrels from local wineries.

BLOOMER CREEK VINEYARDS

5315 Route 414, Hector, NY 14841
Phone: (607) 546-5000
Online: www.bloomercreek.com

The winery takes its name after the rivulet that feeds Cayuga Lake from a spring at the old Bloomer farm. It cuts right through the center of a 10-acre benchland vineyard where Kim Engle practices low-impact farming and manages low crop yields, insuring that each hand-picked cluster of grapes is ripe with intense varietal character. All wines are from sponta-neous fermentations, meaning Kim uses wild yeasts found on the grapes and in the wine cellar. Hard to imagine a more approachable tasting room, housed in a restored Victorian-era carriage house, where well-crafted Pinot Noir, Gamay Noir, Cabernet Franc, and vineyard-designated Rieslings are on display. White wines released under the Tanzen Dame label (homage to the styles of Germany and Alsace) deserve special atten-tion. You might just find the mustachioed Mr. Engle himself pouring your tastings. The people who discover his wines come back vintage after vintage, and that's exactly the idea.

RED NEWT CELLARS

3675 Tichenor Road (off Route 414), Hector, NY 14841
Phone: (607) 546-4100
Online: www.rednewt.com

One glaring oddity is the fact that Red Newt does not own any vineyards and must purchase all its grapes. However, long-term contracts with dependable growers provide exceptional fruit to confident winemaker David Whiting. The winery produces more than a dozen reds and whites, but its reputation stands on the shoulders of Riesling, the grape that best defines the winery. One of the best things about Riesling is that it's possible to experience its unique character even in the less expensive bottlings. Best buy is the "Circle" Riesling, a blend of several vineyard plots with fermentation stopped at varying sugar levels, crafted to medium sweetness with vibrant acid providing balance and structure.

SHALESTONE VINEYARDS

9681 Route 414, Lodi, NY 14860
Phone: (607) 582-6600
Online: www.shalestonevineyards.com

Shalestone is a small winery with a big reputation. Artisan winemaker Rob Thomas has achieved stature in the industry and a loyal following with the mantra, "Red is all we do," a symbol of artistic individualism and a unique niche among the region's producers. Rob handcrafts no more than 10,000 bottles of red wine varietals and creative blends each year, including an interesting Lemberger-Merlot-Syrah proprietary blend cheekily called "Lemberghini." His rich, concentrated beauties are as close as we come to cult wines in the Finger Lakes.

DAÑO'S ON SENECA

9564 Route 414, Lodi, NY 14860
Phone: (607) 582-7555
Online: www.danosonseneca.com
Hours: Wednesday thru Monday, 12 Noon to 9 PM
Corkage Fee: $15

You brush past the chef's herb garden and peer into his kitchen as you enter the restaurant. Daño Hutnik is a superb chef who has played a major role in making the Finger Lakes a food as well as a wine region. The stage of his Austrian wine garden-inspired eatery features sleek counters stacked with pastries and filled with platters of rustic salads and main dishes. Daňo's on Seneca is a Finger Lakes translation of the convivial roadside taverns (heurigers) in the wine-growing regions around Vienna. Servers help you assemble a meal to suit your appetite which you can enjoy inside the charming space or on an open-air patio with a view of the lake. Sip the house wine served in glass mugs (viertels) and forget the cares of the world.

SILVER THREAD VINEYARD

Caywood Road (off Route 414), Lodi, NY 14860
Phone: (607) 582-6116
Online: www.silverthreadwine.com

Silver Thread falls into the select pilgrimage category. Follow the narrow, unpaved end of Caywood Road heading down toward the lake to one of the smaller, more personal wineries, producing small quantities of Chardonnay, Gewurztraminer, Pinot Noir, and exceptional estate-grown and outsourced single-vineyard Rieslings. Paul Brock (M.S. in Enology and Viticulture from Cornell and former winemaker at Lamoreaux Landing) continues progressive pioneer Richard Figiel's sustainable farming practices and hand-crafted wine production.

WAGNER VINEYARDS

9322 Route 414, Lodi, NY 14860
Phone: (607) 582-6450
Online: www.wagnervineyards.com

If the Finger Lakes were a dartboard, Wagner Vineyards would most likely be its bulls-eye, equidistant from all corners of the region — rather fitting, since this enterprise played a central role in the early growth and development of the region's wine industry. Bill Wagner's vision was to create wines that belong in the company of the great wines of the world. By almost any measure, he succeeded in making that vision a reality. His octagonal building is a Finger Lakes landmark. The winery produces a total of thirty wines, all from the estate's 240 acres of vineyards, and all over the varietal map. Focus is on the award-winning Rieslings — dry, semi-dry, sweet, sparkling, and ice wines (most with practical screw caps).

Best of all, the tasting experience here is one of the best educational opportunities in the region. The adjacent microbrewery offers six standard brews in addition to seasonal specialties.

LAMOREAUX LANDING WINE CELLARS

9224 Route 414, Lodi, NY 14860
Phone: (607) 582-6011
Online: www.lamoreauxwine.com

There are several novel aspects to this enterprise, not the least of which is the towering Greco-modern winery, designed by architect Bruce Corson and built in 1992. With a spectacular view of the vineyard hillside and lake, it suggests a cross between Greek Revival architecture, common throughout the Finger Lakes, and one of the region's field barns. One of the most-respected growers in the region, Mark Wagner's vineyards are separated into 20 intensely-managed blocks. Site-to-site comparison is interesting among the winery's single-vineyard Rieslings. Taking inspiration from a common practice in the French Loire, his T23 Cabernet Franc is fermented and aged in stainless-steel tanks.

>Route 414 becomes Route 96A. Follow Route 96A heading north to Geneva.

VENTOSA VINEYARDS

3440 Route 96A, Geneva, NY 14456
Phone: (315) 719-0000
Online: www.ventosavineyards.com

His grandparents grew grapes in the wine region of southern Italy. Lenny Cecere made a fortune building theme parks and commercial water parks around the world. Retired in 1997, he purchased a 107-year-old Geneva farmhouse on 65 acres that was in foreclosure, turning the land into vineyards, winemaking facility, and tasting room to showcase an interesting range of wines. Ventosa (Italian for "windy") offers several Old World-influenced wines fashioned from well-tended vines. This is the place to taste Sangiovese, a rare varietal in the region, as well as the region's only plantings of Tocai Friulano, a Northern Italian classic called "the wine that makes friends easily."

>*At the intersection of 96A and Routes 5&20, make a left turn onto Routes 5&20, turn right onto Castle Street, then left onto Linden Street.*

MICROCLIMATE WINE BAR ⓨ

38 Linden Street, Geneva, NY 14456
Phone: (315) 787-0077
Online: www.facebook.com/microclimatewinebar
Sunday Hours: 5 PM to 10 PM

You'll have to hunt for this place, tucked away on a one-way side street. But what a find! Step up to the curved, sheet metal-topped bar or sink into one of the couches at this countrified wine bar and choose from a range of tasting flights that each pit a Finger Lakes varietal against its counterpart from other points on the globe. How will a local Riesling compare to a German, French, or Australian Riesling? Here's an opportunity to judge for yourself. Nibble on local cheeses, charcuterie.

>*Get back to Routes 5&20 via Castle Street, turn right heading west. Follow signs to Route 14 heading south.*

GENEVA ON THE LAKE ⓧ ⓗ

1001 Lochland Road (Route 14), Geneva, NY 14456
Phone: (315) 789-7190
Online: www.genevaonthelake.com
Corkage Fee: $17

One of the genuine treats of the Finger Lakes. Built in 1914 as a private home and modeled after the Lancelotti villa in the hills of Frascati near Rome, its interior includes Italian marble fireplaces, tapestries, Ionic columns and wood-coffered ceilings. The villa later became a monastery, and then, in 1981, a boutique hotel, managed with impeccable expertise by Bill Schickel. The Lancellotti Dining Room provides a courtly setting for candlelight dinner (local wine-pairing flight available). Flaming desserts served tableside. The mood brightens in summer when the doors are thrown open for patio dining. After a stroll amid spectacular lakeside gardens and classical sculptures, settle in to one of the suites or studios appointed with Stickley furniture. The period atmosphere evokes a gentler time, and it is very easy to get lost in the moment here.

Entry Point:

HAMMONDSPORT

(SOUTH - WEST)

WINE TRAILS

DAY TRIP

KEUKA ARTISAN BAKERY & DELI

49 Shethar Street, Hammondsport, NY 14840
Phone: (607) 224-4001
Online: www.keukaartisanbakery.com
Breakfast Hours: 7 AM to 11 AM

Just steps from the village square, the aroma of fresh-baked breads and sweets will stop you in your tracks. The breads enclose breakfast sandwiches and are toasted to accompany omelets-of-the-day. Save room for dessert from the pastry counter with locally-roasted coffee or espresso, and don't forget to take along a warm-out-of-the-oven baguette to support your day of wine tasting.

PULTENEY SQUARE

Picturesque Hammondsport, on the south end of the lake, has a long history as a vintner's enclave. The first wine grapes in the Finger Lakes were cultivated here in 1829 by William Bostwick, minister of St. James Episcopal Church, and commercial wine production began here in 1860. Many of the fine homes along Lake Street were built by winery owners and winemakers during the second half of the 19th century. Take a morning stroll around the village square of "the Coolest Small Town in America," according to *Budget Travel Magazine.*

>Take Route 54A (Pulteney Street) heading north out of the village, then bear left onto G. H. Taylor Memorial Drive.

BULLY HILL VINEYARDS

8843 G. H. Taylor Memorial Drive, Hammondsport, NY 14840
Phone: (607) 868-3610
Online: www.bullyhill.com

Bully Hill's founder, Walter Taylor, was a larger-than-life character in a sweeping epic of Finger Lakes Wine Country. The grandson of the founder of the Taylor Wine Company and an eager provocateur, Walter railed against the "wine factory" the company had become by the time it was swallowed up by Coca-Cola in 1977. He was a marketing genius whose sense of humor provided an antidote to wine snobbery. While the rascally, holy-terror personality of Walter Taylor is gone from his beloved winery, his anti-establishment wine making and off-the-wall labels have earned him a hero's status in the Finger Lakes. Visit here, if only to soak up a bit of the lore of the legendary "Baron of Bully Hill" and champion of the less sophisticated palate. With one of the most extensive list of wines (and labels) in the region, there's an air of amusement park excitement here, and few Finger Lakes wineries are busier on a summer day than Bully Hill.

GREYTON H. TAYLOR WINE MUSEUM

Greyton H. Taylor Memorial Drive, Hammondsport, NY 14840
Phone: (607) 868-4814
Online: www.bullyhill.com/museum/museum.asp

On the grounds of Bully Hill Vineyards, the first wine museum in America is devoted to the Taylor family endeavor that began in 1878. The Cooper Shop Building includes local memorabilia and wine making equipment from the early days of the Finger Lakes wine industry. The Art Gallery houses original artwork by Walter S. Taylor artifacts from the days of Prohibition, presidential glassware, and a collection of Taylor family photos.

>*Take Sanford Road to Route 76. Turn left, heading north.*

HERON HILL WINERY

9301 Route 76, Hammondsport, NY 14840
Phone: (800) 441-4241
Online: www.heronhill.com

What began as the 1977 winegrowing endeavor of John and Josephine Ford Ingle (she is the great-granddaughter of Henry Ford) has become one of the region's most prominent wineries. In 2000, the winery was transformed into an architecturally flamboyant, state-of-the-art facility, a postmodern edifice with rounded, vaulted ceilings suggestive of a giant wine barrel and a tasting room that seems more like a sleek nightclub bar. With some of the area's most impressive views of the vineyards and Keuka Lake, Heron Hill was chosen as one of the ten most spectacular tasting rooms in the world by *Travel + Leisure*. The wine portfolio offers nearly 20 varieties, from crisp, light Rieslings to aromatic, dry Chardonnays. Most noteworthy are Rieslings from the family-farmed Ingle Vineyard.

>*Continue north on Route 76, then bear right onto Middle Road.*

DR. FRANK'S VINIFERA WINE CELLARS

9749 Middle Road (off Route 76), Hammondsport, NY 14840
Phone: (800) 320-0735
Online: www.drfrankwines.com

The Frank family is the closest we have to royalty in the Finger Lakes. Fred, president and general manager is now entrusted to preserve the historical accomplishments of his grandfather, Konstantin Frank, the Ukrainian-born doctor of enology who is credited with changing the course of winegrowing in the Finger Lakes. *Wine Report* named Dr. Frank Cellars the "Greatest Wine Producer in the Northeast." In the 1950s, Dr. Frank planted an old, winter-hardy, German Riesling clone, prized for its low yields of intensely aromatic and flavorful fruit with classic mineral notes, and the wines here behave as German Rieslings typically do. Not only are they deliciously vivacious in their youth, they continue drinking well as they become complex and more-nuanced with age. Willy Frank, Fred's father, called the older Rieslings his "Marlene Dietrich wines." You may end up drinking some of the best wines on the planet here, and in surely one of the prettiest places it's grown. Take home an "educational case."

>*Double back to the village heading south on Route 76, pick up Route 54 heading up along the eastern shore of Keuka Lake (about 30 minutes).*

SWITZERLAND INN

14109 Keuka Village Road (Route 54), Hammondsport, NY 14840
Phone: (607) 292-6927
Online: www.theswitz.com
Corkage Fee: $10

This sprawling, multi-level old dame shows her age in places. Hugging the eastern shore of the lake, "the Switz" has been in continuous operation since 1894. Ask for a table on the deck overlooking the lake, and order from a menu of soups, salads, burgers, sandwiches, pizza, and fish fry.

RAVINES WINE CELLARS 🍷

14630 Route 54, Hammondsport, NY 14840
Phone: (315) 781-7007
Online: www.ravineswinecellars.com

French wine lovers worship the land, but in the Finger Lakes, the wine-maker is king. Morten Hallgren was raised among the casks and vines of his family's winemaking estate in Provence, so the French influence is strong here, both in the wines and the winery. You might say that Morten is to the Riesling grape what Yo-Yo Ma is to the cello. For his exquisite, Alsace-inspired Rieslings, he purchases a spectrum of grapes from a range of sites, convincing growers to lower croploads for more concentrated, complex wines. Grapes are whole bunch pressed to ensure gentle extraction of flavor compounds, retaining delicate fruit characters, floral and mineral elements. Deposits of residual yeast are stirred at the end of fermentation, a technique the French refer to as battonage, to soften acidity. Ravines was recently named by *Wine Spectator* among the 100 best wineries in the world. (Wine tastings include chocolate and cheese pairings).

>*Follow Route 54 heading south, turn right onto 54A, then left onto Lake Street (Pleasant Valley Road).*

PLEASANT VALLEY WINE COMPANY 🍷

8260 Pleasant Valley Road, Hammondsport, NY 14840
Phone: (607) 569-6111
Online: www.pleasantvalleywine.com

The past is prologue, so an understanding of Finger Lakes wine culture wouldn't be complete without a visit here. The Pleasant Valley Wine Company is now home to the Great Western, Gold Seal, and Widmer brands, once mighty giants in the wine industry. The 25-minute tour includes a bus ride to the original 1860 Great Western facility (Bonded Winery No. 1) and a display of artifacts from early winemaking in the region. Even the wines are museum pieces, most made with native variety grapes, now out of favor as drinkers become more sophisticated in their taste preferences.

>*Take Lake Street (Pleasant Valley Road) back into the village. Make a right turn onto Route 54A, then another right onto Route 54 heading south.*

FINGER LAKES BEER COMPANY 🍺

8462 New York 54, Hammondsport, NY 14840
Phone: (607) 569-3311
Online: www.fingerlakesbeercompany.com

Sometimes going against the grain is a good thing. In 2010, amateur brewers and avid craft beer enthusiasts Wayne Peworchik and Mark Goodwin established this microbrewery smack dab in what has always been known as wine country. Yet both locals and tourists have proved equally gregarious beer drinkers, keeping the tap room hopping as the range of offerings evolves and becomes more sophisticated. Sample year-round standbys Copper Ale and Hammonds-Porter (brewed with chocolate malt and vanilla beans), and a seasonal wheat beer brewed with fresh watermelon. All beers travel in growlers or bottles.

>*Take Route 54 heading north, make a left turn, following Route 54A into the village*

THE VILLAGE TAVERN 🍴

30 Mechanic Street (on Pulteney Square), Hammondsport, NY 14840
Phone: (607) 569-2528
Online: www.villagetaverninn.com
Hours: Daily, 5 PM to 9 PM (Memorial Day to October 31); Call for off-season schedule
Corkage Policy: No outside wine allowed

Winery folks have made the Village Tavern their central gathering place, but anyone feels welcome. Careful not to drop the wine list on your foot, as you could really hurt yourself. One of the thrills of eating here is the opportunity to browse through the encyclopedic, all-Finger Lakes wine list, novel for both its breadth and entertainment value. The ambitious dinner menu offers a bit of something for everyone.

>*Take Route 54A heading east, then right onto Route 54.*

PLEASANT VALLEY INN 🛏

7979 Route 54, Hammondsport, NY 14840
Phone: (607) 569-2282
Online: www.pleasantvalleyinn.com

The tavern room is the perfect spot for an after dinner brandy by the fireplace before retiring to one of the four guest rooms (queen-size beds with private baths) in this charming county inn. Weather permitting, continental breakfast is served on the patio overlooking the surrounding vineyards. (Open May thru November)

Entry Point:

HAMMONDSPORT

(SOUTH - WEST)

WINE TRAILS

WEEKEND TOUR

Friday

THE VILLAGE TAVERN

30 Mechanic Street (on Pulteney Square), Hammondsport, NY 14840
Phone: (607) 569-2528
Online: www.villagetaverninn.com
Hours: Daily, 5 PM to 9 PM (Memorial Day to October 31); Call for off-season schedule
Corkage Policy: No outside wine allowed

Winery folks have made the Village Tavern their central gathering place, but anyone feels welcome. Careful not to drop the wine list on your foot, as you could really hurt yourself. One of the thrills of eating here is the opportunity to browse through the encyclopedic, all-Finger Lakes wine list, novel for both its breadth and entertainment value. The ambitious dinner menu offers a bit of something for everyone.

KEUKA LAKESIDE INN

24 Water Street, Hammondsport, NY 14840
Phone: (607) 569-2600
Online: www.keukalakesideinn.com

It's all about the view at this updated, old-style motel perched at the water's edge and just a short walk from the village square. At the end of the day, relax in the gazebo and contemplate the serene waters of Keuka, the name the Seneca people gave to the lake for their "canoe landing."

Saturday

KEUKA ARTISAN BAKERY & DELI

49 Shethar Street, Hammondsport, NY 14840
Phone: (607) 224-4001
Online: www.keukaartisanbakery.com
Breakfast Hours: 7 AM to 11 AM

Just steps from the village square, the aroma of fresh-baked breads and

sweets will stop you in your tracks. The breads enclose breakfast sandwiches and are toasted to accompany omelets-of-the-day. Save room for
dessert from the pastry counter with locally-roasted coffee or espresso,
and don't forget to take along a warm-out-of-the-oven baguette to support
your day of wine tasting.

PULTENEY SQUARE

Picturesque Hammondsport, on the south end of the lake, has a long history as a vintner's enclave. The first wine grapes in the Finger Lakes were
cultivated here in 1829 by William Bostwick, minister of St. James Episcopal Church, and commercial wine production began here in 1860. Many
of the fine homes along Lake Street were built by winery owners and
winemakers during the second half of the 19th century. Take a stroll
around the village square of "the Coolest Small Town in America," according to *Budget Travel Magazine*.

>*Take Route 54A (Pulteney Street) heading north out of the village, then
bear left onto G. H. Taylor Memorial Drive.*

BULLY HILL VINEYARDS

8843 G. H. Taylor Memorial Drive, Hammondsport, NY 14840
Phone: (607) 868-3610
Online: www.bullyhill.com

Bully Hill's founder, Walter Taylor, was a larger-than-life character in a
sweeping epic of Finger Lakes Wine Country. The grandson of the founder of the Taylor Wine Company and an eager provocateur, Walter railed
against the "wine factory" the company had become by the time it was
swallowed up by Coca-Cola in 1977. He was a marketing genius whose
sense of humor provided an antidote to wine snobbery. While the rascally, holy-terror personality of Walter Taylor is gone from his beloved winery, his anti-establishment wine making and off-the-wall labels have
earned him a hero's status in the Finger Lakes. Visit here, if only to soak
up a bit of the lore of the legendary "Baron of Bully Hill" and champion of
the less sophisticated palate. With one of the most extensive list of wines
(and labels) in the region, there's an air of amusement park excitement
here, and few Finger Lakes wineries are busier on a summer day than
Bully Hill.

GREYTON H. TAYLOR WINE MUSEUM 🔭

Greyton H. Taylor Memorial Drive, Hammondsport, NY 14840
Phone: (607) 868-4814
Online: www.bullyhill.com/museum/museum.asp

On the grounds of Bully Hill Vineyards, the first wine museum in America is devoted to the Taylor family endeavor that began in 1878. The Cooper Shop Building includes local memorabilia and wine making equipment from the early days of the Finger Lakes wine industry. The Art Gallery houses original artwork by Walter S. Taylor artifacts from the days of Prohibition, presidential glassware, and a collection of Taylor family photos.

>*Take Sanford Road to Route 76. Turn left, heading north.*

HERON HILL WINERY 🍷

9301 Route 76, Hammondsport, NY 14840
Phone: (800) 441-4241
Online: www.heronhill.com

What began as the 1977 winegrowing endeavor of John and Josephine Ford Ingle (she is the great-granddaughter of Henry Ford) has become one of the region's most prominent wineries. In 2000, the winery was transformed into an architecturally flamboyant, state-of-the-art facility, a postmodern edifice with rounded, vaulted ceilings suggestive of a giant wine barrel and a tasting room that seems more like a sleek nightclub bar. With some of the area's most impressive views of the vineyards and Keuka Lake, Heron Hill was chosen as one of the ten most spectacular tasting rooms in the world by *Travel + Leisure.* The wine portfolio offers nearly 20 varieties, from crisp, light Rieslings to aromatic, dry Chardonnays. Most noteworthy are Rieslings from the family-farmed Ingle Vineyard.

>*Continue north on Route 76, then bear right onto Middle Road.*

DR. FRANK'S VINIFERA WINE CELLARS 🍷

9749 Middle Road (off Route 76), Hammondsport, NY 14840
Phone: (800) 320-0735
Online: www.drfrankwines.com

The Frank family is the closest we have to royalty in the Finger Lakes. Fred, president and general manager is now entrusted to preserve the historical accomplishments of his grandfather, Konstantin Frank, the Ukrainian-born doctor of enology who is credited with changing the course of wine growing in the Finger Lakes. *Wine Report* named Dr. Frank Cellars the "Greatest Wine Producer in the Northeast." In the 1950s, Dr. Frank planted an old, winter-hardy, German Riesling clone, prized for its low yields of intensely aromatic and flavorful fruit with classic mineral notes, and the wines here behave as German Rieslings typically do. Not only are they deliciously vivacious in their youth, they continue drinking well as they become complex and more-nuanced with age. Willy Frank, Fred's father, called the older Rieslings his "Marlene Dietrich wines." You may end up drinking some of the best wines on the planet here, and in surely one of the prettiest places it's grown.

>*Continue heading north on Middle Road, make a right turn onto Shuart Road, then a left onto Route 54A heading north along the western shore of the lake (about 15 minutes). Make a left turn onto Italy Hill Road.*

HUNT COUNTRY VINEYARDS ⓨ

4021 Italy Hill Road, Branchport, NY 14418
Phone: (315) 595-2812
Online: www.huntcountryvineyards.com

The vineyards encompass 50 acres of well-tended grapes, crafted into exceptional wines including Chardonnay, Pinot Gris, Cabernet Franc, and Rieslings. But what excels here is the art of sculpting frozen fruit into ice wines, so good they have accompanied dessert at White House dinners. Hardy Vignoles grapes are left on the vines past traditional harvest time so more sugar and interesting characters can develop. When temperatures drop to 20 degrees or below, they are picked by hand, carried to the winery, and pressed immediately, as juice is separated from skin and pulp, drop by drop. They produce a wonderful dessert wine with mouth-filling texture and hints of apricots and tropical fruit. Expect to pay dearly for ice wines, but they are well worth the splurge.

>*Get back onto Route 54A heading north to Bluff Point.*

ESPERANZA MANSION ✍️

3456 Route 54A, Bluff Point, NY 14478
Phone: (315) 536-4400
Online: www.esperanzamansion.com
Hours: Call for seasonal schedule
Corkage Fee: $15

John Nicholas Rose, the son of Robert and Jane Rose, journeyed to the Finger Lakes region from the family plantation in Stafford County, Virginia. He purchased 1,000 acres of land and completed construction of the home he called "Esperanza" (derived from the Latin word for "hope") in 1838. It's a little piece of heaven sitting astride the Keuka highlands — a Greek Revival mansion lovingly restored to its 19th century splendor. Offering three separate dining areas, outdoor terrace and patio seating with a breathtaking view. Put on your sunglasses and grab an outdoor seat. Among the dazzling vistas along Keuka Lake, this place may be the best.

>*Continue on Route 54A heading north.*

YATES CELLARS 🍷

3170 Route 54A, Bluff Point, NY 14478
Phone: (315) 575-1863
Online: www.yatescellars.com

The setting is a stately building, listed on the National Register of Historic Places as the Henry Rose House, Hampstead, just up the road from his brother John's Esperanza Mansion. The 1838 home, surrounded by vineyards that date back to 1860, is now the setting for a winery and tasting parlor. You might just find owner/winemaker Alan Hunt roaming around. Although he sells a lion's share of his 25-acre harvest to Bully Hill, Alan still has plenty of grapes left to make his own wines. Taste the Rieslings.

>*Just past Keuka College, turn left onto Merritt Hill Road.*

ABANDON BREWING COMPANY 🍺

2994 Merritt Hill Road, Penn Yan, NY 14527

Phone: (585) 209-3276
Online: www.abandonbrewing.com

Sheltered in a restored nineteenth-century barn amidst seven acres of vineyards, apple orchards, walnut groves, and a hopyard with six varieties to flavor their beers, this farmhouse brewery is simply a spectacular place to visit, one of the region's charming pastoral retreats. Partner and brewmaster Jeff Hillebrandt interned at Custom Brewcrafters, studied brewing at schools in Chicago and Munich, Germany, then worked for Belgian beer specialist Brewery Ommegang before joining the team at Abandon. The mastery of his profession is on display in a range of undeniably eclectic offerings, many crafted with crops that grow on and around Abandon Acres, including walnuts and black currants. After sampling at the tasting bar, take a pint of your favorite out on the deck overlooking Keuka Lake from the top of Merritt Hill.

>*Get back onto Route 54A; continue heading north to the village of Penn Yan.*

PENN YAN HISTORIC DISTRICT 👀

The name of the village was contrived from the first syllables of "Pennsylvania" and "Yankee," as most of the early settlers were Pennsylvanians and New Englanders (or Yankees). Work up an appetite for dinner. Stroll over to the historic district with a broad range of architecturally significant examples of residential, commercial, industrial, civic and ecclesiastical structures. Highlights include the Birkett Mills, Chronicle Building, Knapp Hotel, and the Castner House.

KEUKA RESTAURANT 🍴

12 Main Street, Penn Yan, NY 14527
Phone: (315) 536-5852
Online: www.keuka-restaurant.com
Hours: Daily, 11 AM to 10 PM
Corkage Fee: $8

You don't come to Penn Yan expecting molecular gastronomy. The food is conservative, small-town, American family restaurant fare, nothing fancy, but it's done properly. The selection of local wines gives a special regional emphasis to the wine list.

SENECA FARMS ICE CREAM

2485 Route 54A, Penn Yan, NY 14527
Phone: (315) 536-4066
Online: www.senecafarmsny.com

When in Penn Yan, do as the locals do. After dinner drive over to this 1950s-era ice cream parlor for a Turtle Sundae with homemade vanilla ice cream, hot fudge and hot caramel sauces, and toasted pecans. (Open March thru end of October)

BEST WESTERN VINEYARD INN & SUITES

142 Lake Street, Penn Yan, NY 14527
Phone: (315) 536-8473
Online: www.vineyardinnandsuites.com

Clean, comfortable, wine-centric hotel within walking distance to downtown with fitness center, indoor heated pool, hot tub and business center. Rooms have a mini-fridge for the wine you purchased earlier in the day.

Sunday

PENN YAN DINER

131 East Elm Street, Penn Yan, NY 14527
Phone: (315) 536-6004
Online: www.pennyandiner.com

Breakfast here isn't anything you can't get most elsewhere, except for the sense of small town charm and the fact that you get to eat in a real diner. It's a genuine slice of Americana, built in 1925 by the Richardson Dining Car factory, the first diner manufacturer in western New York, and it's had a succession of owners over the years, operated since 2012 by Carrie and Sean Ahearn. Freshly-brewed Finger Lakes Coffee Roasters' beans make a damn good cup of diner coffee.

>*Take Route 54 out of the village, heading south along the eastern shore of the lake.*

KEUKA SPRING VINEYARDS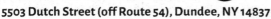

243 East Lake Road (Route 54), Penn Yan, NY 14527
Phone: (315) 536-3147
Online: www.keukaspringwinery.com

The agrarian, wooden winery fits comfortably into the rural setting, providing a pergola and terrace with picnic tables for an unobstructed view of the vineyard and across the lake to Keuka College. Inside the bright and airy tasting room you'll find a knowledgeable and friendly staff happy to pour samples of wines that are fruity, balanced, food-friendly and delicious. If you're unfamiliar with the variety, Keuka Spring may offer the region's best introduction to Lemberger, a cold-hearty Austrian variety that dates back to the days of Napoleon Bonaparte and Otto von Bismarck, both of whom enjoyed the wine. Also noteworthy is a Merlot-Cabernet Sauvignon, red meat-friendly blend called Miller's Cove Red.

ROOSTER HILL VINEYARDS

489 Route 54, Penn Yan, NY 14527
Phone: (315) 536-4773
Online: www.roosterhill.com

The interior is tastefully decorated with straw-colored walls surrounded by copper moulding; the space is highlighted by an oval bar that cleverly provides a lake view to every wine taster. Sample an exceptional Sweet Riesling in one of the prettiest tasting rooms in the Finger Lakes. Its name inspired by a breed of English hen, "Silver Pencil" is a proprietary blend of Vidal Blanc, Seyval Blanc, and Cayuga White grapes. Pick up a couple of bottles to serve as a dinner party aperitif.

>Continue on Route 54 heading south along the eastern shore of Keuka Lake. Turn left onto Hyatt Hill Road, then left onto Dutch Street.

MCGREGOR VINEYARD WINERY

5503 Dutch Street (off Route 54), Dundee, NY 14837
Phone: (607) 292-3999
Online: www.mcgregorwinery.com

Slightly out-of-the-way, but more than worth the effort. One of Keuka

Lake's most venerable producers, the rustic winery has a 1,200-foot perch overlooking Bluff Point at the widest expanse of Keuka Lake. The combination of cool temperatures and significant "lake effect" winds on the steep, north-facing slope stresses the vines, produces smaller yields, and results in more mature and concentrated flavors in the grapes. Semi-sweet Riesling is a long-standing success story, and the winery makes its mark on Finger Lakes viticulture with plantings of rare, Eastern-European wine grapes, propagated from a mother lode of cuttings that originated in the former Soviet Republic of Georgia. Two hardy varieties with noble bloodlines, Saperavi and Sereksia Charni, are married to produce an audacious red wine called "Black Russian."

>*Go back to Route 54 heading south and watch for Switzerland Inn on the right.*

SWITZERLAND INN

14109 Keuka Village Road (off Route 54), Hammondsport, NY 14840
Phone: (607) 292-6927
Online: www.theswitz.com
Corkage Fee: $10

This sprawling, multi-level old dame shows her age in places. Hugging the eastern shore of Keuka Lake, "the Switz" has been in continuous operation since 1894. Ask for a table on the deck overlooking the lake, and order from a menu of soups, salads, burgers, sandwiches, pizza, and fish fry.

RAVINES WINE CELLARS

14630 Route 54, Hammondsport, NY 14840
Phone: (315) 781-7007
Online: www.ravineswinecellars.com

French wine lovers worship the land, but in the Finger Lakes, the wine-maker is king. Morten Hallgren was raised among the casks and vines of his family's winemaking estate in Provence, so the French influence is strong here, both in the wines and the winery. You might say that Morten is to the Riesling grape what Yo-Yo Ma is to the cello. For his exquisite, Alsace-inspired Rieslings, he purchases a spectrum of grapes from a range of sites, convincing growers to lower croploads for more concentrated, complex wines. Grapes are whole bunch pressed to ensure gentle extraction of flavor compounds, retaining delicate fruit characters, floral and mineral elements. Deposits of residual yeast are stirred at the end of fermentation, a technique the French refer to as battonage, to soften acidity. Ravines was recently named by *Wine Spectator* among the 100 best wineries in the world. (Wine tastings include chocolate and cheese pairings).

>*Follow Route 54 heading south, turn right onto 54A, then left onto Lake Street (Pleasant Valley Road).*

PLEASANT VALLEY WINE COMPANY

8260 Pleasant Valley Road, Hammondsport, NY 14840
Phone: (607) 569-6111
Online: www.pleasantvalleywine.com

The past is prologue, so an understanding of Finger Lakes wine culture wouldn't be complete without a visit here. The Pleasant Valley Wine Company is now home to the Great Western, Gold Seal, and Widmer brands, once mighty giants in the wine industry. The 25-minute tour includes a bus ride to the original 1860 Great Western facility (Bonded Winery No. 1) and a display of artifacts from early winemaking in the region. Even the wines are museum pieces, most made with native variety grapes, now out of favor as drinkers become more sophisticated in their taste preferences.

>*Follow Lake Street (Pleasant Valley Road) back into the village. Make a right turn onto Route 54A, then another right onto Route 54 heading south.*

FINGER LAKES BEER COMPANY

8462 New York 54, Hammondsport, NY 14840
Phone: (607) 569-3311
Online: www.fingerlakesbeercompany.com

You're probably up to here in wine, so take an opportunity to cleanse the palate and prepare your taste buds for dinner. In 2010, homebrewers and avid craft beer enthusiasts Wayne Peworchik and Mark Goodwin established this microbrewery smack dab in what has always been known as

wine country. Yet both locals and tourists have proved equally gregarious beer drinkers, keeping the tap room hopping as the range of offerings
evolves and becomes more sophisticated. Sample year-round standbys
Copper Ale and Hammonds-Porter (brewed with chocolate malt and vanilla beans), and a seasonal wheat beer brewed with fresh watermelon.
All beers travel in growlers or bottles.

>*Continue on Route 54 heading south.*

PLEASANT VALLEY INN 🍴 🛏

7979 Route 54, Hammondsport, NY 14840
Phone: (607) 569-2282
Online: www.pleasantvalleyinn.com
Hours: Thursday thru Sunday, 5 PM to 9 PM
Corkage Fee: $15

When folks come to wine country, they expect to find picturesque set-
tings, regionally-influenced cuisine with a deep local wine list, and gra-
cious hospitality. Every expectation is fulfilled at Tom and Marianne
Simons' homey, easygoing spot, where the dishes are uncomplicated and
satisfying. The tavern room is the perfect spot for an after dinner brandy
by the fireplace, then retire to one of the four inviting guest rooms, all
queen-size with private baths. A European-style continental breakfast
will be ready in the morning. (Open May thru November)

Entry Point:

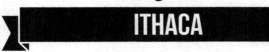

ITHACA

(SOUTH - EAST)

WINE TRAILS

DAY TRIP

ITHACA BAKERY 🍴 🛒

400 North Meadow Street (Route 13 North), Ithaca, NY 14850
Phone: (607) 273-7110
Online: www.ithacabakery.com

Hobnob with the locals at Ithaca Bakery. Turning out 1,000 bagels a day, along with artisan breads and pastries, the bakery is also a cafe, deli, and the best place to kick off your day. Nibble from the self-service breakfast buffet bar and pick up picnic fixings for later — glass display cases are loaded with prepared entrees and side dishes.

>From the bakery parking lot, turn right, then left onto Route 13 South, then immediately right to Route 96; pick up Route 89 North along the western shore of Cayuga Lake.

TAUGHANNOCK FALLS 🔭

While it's not exactly in your travel pattern, you shouldn't miss this natural wonder. Take a short drive off Route 89 onto Taughannock Park Road to gawk at New York State's highest waterfall, dropping 215 feet past rocky cliffs that tower nearly 400 feet above the gorge, making it 33 feet taller than Niagara Falls and one of the largest single-drop waterfalls east of the Rocky Mountains. Gorge and rim trails provide spectacular views of the falls from above and below. Visitors in autumn can enjoy the picturesque colors of the surrounding trees. The adjacent park offers hiking and nature trails, camping, picnicking, swimming, fishing, and a boat launch.

>Go back to Route 89 heading north along the western shore of Cayuga Lake.

FRONTENAC POINT VINEYARD 🍷

9501 Route 89, Trumansburg, NY 14886
Phone: (607) 387-9619
Online: www.frontenacpoint.com

Hours are somewhat irregular here, so call ahead. Owner/winemaker Jim Doolittle shows success with an often-ignored grape variety called Chambourcin, dominating the Frontenac Point portfolio with no less than five wines produced from the versatile grape. While some hybrid flavors, especially among the reds, will challenge a palate accustomed to viniferas, in the right hands Chamboursin is an exception. As a varietal, it develops into a tasty, dark and fresh dark purple wine exhibiting ripe mulberry, elderberry, and black cherry flavors, with underlying herbaceous notes. Admirers of full bodied, fruit driven wines will appreciate the extra time (up to 4 years) that goes into the aging of Proprietor's Reserve before release. (Don't miss the 10-foot-tall, wind-driven sound sculpture installed on the bow of the winery deck overlooking Cayuga Lake).

BELLWETHER CIDERY 🍷

9070 Route 89, Trumansburg, NY 14886
Phone: (607) 387-9464
Online: www.cidery.com

The wide choice of locally-grown apples gives Bellwether cidermaker Bill Barton a lot to work with, and the results are exceptional varietals and blends. Many of his ciders are concocted from varieties usually considered "eating apples." Empire, Gala, and Fuji are combined in the semi-dry "Original" Hard Cider. "Liberty Spy" has a hearty taste and succulent mouthfeel from the blend of Liberty and Northern Spy apples; the marriage of local Tompkins King and Baldwin produces a tart, refreshing quaff called "King Baldwin." Bellwether's Heritage Hard Cider includes up to 25 varieties of bittersweets and bittersharps (with names like Somerset Redstreak, Tremlett's Bitter, Harry Masters Jersey, and Brown Snout) for a full-bodied drink of rich complexity. Bellwether Wine Cellars, an offshoot of the cidery, focuses on Riesling and Pinot Noir made from field- and table-sorted Keuka and Seneca Lake-sourced fruit.

SHELDRAKE POINT VINEYARD 🍷

7448 County Road 153 (off Route 89), Ovid, NY 14521
Phone: (607) 532-9401
Online: www.sheldrakepoint.com

A winery with a good backstory. This remarkable enterprise hugs the shore at Cayuga Lake's deepest point, creating a microclimate that lengthens the growing season up to two weeks longer than many other areas in the Finger Lakes. After earning a graduate degree from the Cornell Hotel School in 1994, Chuck Tauck joined an adventurous group of people who converted one of the Point's old dairy farms into a vineyard planted with rows of Riesling, Chardonnay, Gewurztraminer, Pinot Gris, Pinot Noir, Gamay, Merlot, Cabernet Franc, and Cabernet Sauvignon grapes, covering nearly 50 acres. Fantastically rich in fruit flavors, the Sheldrake portfolio of Rieslings, from dry to semi-dry to ice wine, demonstrates that world-class Rieslings have arrived in the Finger Lakes.

THIRSTY OWL WINE COMPANY

6799 Elm Beach Road (off Route 89), Ovid, NY 14521
Phone: (607) 869-5805
Online: www.thirstyowl.com

When Jonathan Cupp purchased a parcel of the former Plane family estate in 2001, he inherited the oldest Riesling vines on Cayuga Lake. Dr. Robert Plane, educator and viticulturalist, planted noble Rieslings on this site in 1972, and after three decades, each drop of wine reflects the character of its grapevine's maturity, so it comes as no surprise that Thirsty Owl bottles regularly capture prestigious medals at wine competitions. Just off the tasting room, the bistro menu offers a range of well-prepared, wine-friendly small plates, salads, flatbreads, and sandwiches.

CAYUGA RIDGE ESTATE WINERY

Address: 6800 Route 89, Ovid, NY 14521
Phone: (607) 869-5158
Online: www.cayugaridgewinery.com

Most hybrid grapes were developed by French scientists between 1880 and 1950. Their goal was to combine the finer taste characteristics of European vinifera varieties with the winter-hardiness and disease-resistance of the Native-American varieties. Hybrid varieties continue to be developed specifically for the Finger Lakes and other cool climate regions at Cornell University's New York State Agricultural Experiment Station. The grand old cavernous barn at Cayuga Ridge provides a rustic setting for tasting a range of good to terrific wines, in particular, Cayuga White, a regional hybrid cross, developed at the Experiment Station in 1972. The mother-block of Cayuga White at Cayuga Ridge, blanketing 8 acres of the vineyard with vigorous clusters of greenish-gold, translucent grapes is entrusted to Tom Challen, a skilled grower and winemaker from

Canadian wine country. It's an easy-to-enjoy "sipping wine," often compared to Pinot Grigio. Wood-fired pizzas offered here on summer weekends, Fridays, Saturdays and Sundays from 11:30 AM to 5:30 PM.

HOSMER WINERY ⑦

6999 Route 89, Ovid, NY 14521
Phone: (607) 869-3393
Online: www.hosmerwinery.com

Dedicated to the respected European concept of making wine only from his own vineyards, Cameron "Tunker" Hosmer was one of the region's earliest believers in Cabernet Franc as a varietal, and his winery boasts some of the best in the region; some say it's one of the finest in America. His vines receive treatment more reminiscent of gardening than viticulture, and it shows, not only in Cab Franc, but with distinctive Rieslings (from 30 years old vines planted on high-lime Cazenovia loam soils).

>Reverse course and follow Route 89 heading south to Ithaca. Turn right onto State Street, then left onto Brindley Street. Cross the one lane bridge and drive to the corner of Taber Street.

PORTS OF NEW YORK ⑦

815 Taber Street, Ithaca, NY 14850
Phone: (607) 220-6317
Online: www.portsofnewyork.com

Hightail it back to Ithaca for a visit to what is not only the region's most eccentric winery, it's a treasure trove of history. Frédéric Bouché contracts for premium local grapes to make fortified, Port-inspired wines at an enterprise that doubles as a museum of sorts. Frédéric is on hand to pour tastings of his handcrafted wines and tell stories about the vintage winemaking tools he inherited from La Maison Bouché, the winery his family established in Normandy in 1919.

>Continue on Taber Street, make a left onto Cecil Malone Drive, then another left onto Route 13 heading north. Turn right onto 3rd Street, then left onto Franklin Street.

RED FEET WINE MARKET & SPIRIT PROVISIONS

435 Franklin Street, Ithaca, NY 14850
Phone: (607) 330-1056
Online: www.redfeetwine.com

If you're still in the market for something to take home, stop in and browse this boutique wine shop, a serious yet unintimidating place for wine lovers. Dewi Rainey and her knowledgeable staff are big supporters of Finger Lakes wines, offering a diverse, thoughtfully-curated selection, displayed right up front. Prices are across the board.

>*Make a left turn onto Route 13 heading south and turn left onto West State Street.*

MAXIE'S SUPPER CLUB & OYSTER BAR

635 West State Street (at Route 13 South), Ithaca, NY 14850
Phone: (607) 272-4136
Online: www.maxies.com
Corkage Fee: $15

The ramshackle, romper-room décor of this loveable, offbeat joint belies the seriousness of the food. Once you get past the cheerful artificiality of Mardi Gras masks, beads and the purple mise-en-scène, you can settle in for Maxie's brand of New Orleans cuisine, a dig-on-in approach to supper in Ithaca with casual but intelligent service and food bursting with flavor. The menu sprawls from bar bites to full entrees, mostly true to NOLA's culinary art form. Maxie's cellar is woefully understocked with local wines, so you might consider dinner here an opportunity to try one of the dependable beer offerings on tap, always cold, fresh, and very good with bartender-shucked oysters (half-price during Happy Hour).

>*Follow State Street east to the Commons. Turn right, then left onto Green Street. Follow Green Street to the merge with East State Street.*

BAR ARGOS

408 East State Street, Ithaca, NY 14850
Phone: (607) 319-4437
Online: www.argosinn.com

For an after-dinner drink, head across town. Ensconced in the Argos Inn, a 10-room B&B, this temple to the obsessively crafted cocktail has become a cult favorite among locals.

>*Drive west on State Street, turn left onto South Aurora Street (becoming Route 96B) and continue up South Hill.*

LA TOURELLE 🛏️

1150 Danby Road (Route 96B), Ithaca, NY 14850
Phone: (800) 765-1492
Online: www.latourelle.com

This lovely retreat is nestled on seventy rolling acres just past Ithaca College, atop South Hill. Expertly managed by Scott Wiggins, La Tourelle pampers guests with feather beds in well-appointed rooms. The property includes 4 tennis courts, hiking trails, and spa with a range of services including "vino-therapy" (powdered regional grape seeds rubbed into the skin).

Pitched on the grounds of La Tourelle, Firelight Camps provides an overnight experience for the more adventurous. It's called "glamping" (glamorous camping). Sleep outdoors in a safari tent and awaken to a continental breakfast with locally-roasted "campfire coffee." More info at www.firelightcamps.com.

Entry Point:

ITHACA

(SOUTH - EAST)

WINE TRAILS

WEEKEND TOUR

Friday

THE CELLAR D'OR 🛒

136 Ithaca Commons, Ithaca, NY 14850
Phone: (607) 319-0500
Online: www.thecellardor.com

Like many small towns with attitude, Ithaca has a downtown "mall" called the Commons. Browse a few of the eclectic shops, then duck into this wine boutique, specializing in small production estate-bottled wines and ciders. Free wine tastings offered every Friday from 5 to 7 PM.

JUST A TASTE 🍴

116 North Aurora Street, Ithaca, NY 14850
Phone: (607) 277-9463
Online: www.just-a-taste.com
Corkage Fee: $15.

Don't be dismayed if there's a long line at Just a Taste, tables turn over quickly. Working from a kitchen space only slightly larger than a mop closet, chef/owner Jen Irwin and her team create a nightly-changing profusion of locally-inspired tapas and raciones (larger portions of the tapas), so you can eat and share as much or as little as you like without having the formality of a typical dinner. The waitstaff is as accomplished as the cuisine, borderline compulsive when it comes to clearing your table, making room before the next dish arrives. Wine is a passion, and there is passion here aplenty. Sample from 45 rotating wines by the glass or "tasting glass" or in flights of five wines, including a dependable "Local Flight." Ah, decisions, decisions.

HILTON GARDEN INN 🛏️ 🛒

130 E. Seneca Street, Ithaca, NY 14850
Phone: (607) 277-8900
Online: www.hiltongardeninn.com

104 comfortable guestrooms in downtown Ithaca (just around the corner from Just a Taste) each equipped with work desk, high-speed internet

access, microwave and refrigerator. No need to use the in-room coffee-maker, there's a Starbucks at street level. The hotel provides a downtown home to Sarah's Patisserie, a sweet little gem where French-inspired pastries and chocolates are hand-crafted by owner Tammy Travis, who followed studies at the French Culinary Institute in NYC with a position as pastry assistant to esteemed chocolatier Jacques Torres. It would be a shame to abstain.

Saturday

ITHACA FARMERS MARKET ✍ 🛒

545 Third Street, Ithaca, NY 14850
Phone: (607) 273-7109
Online: www.ithacamarket.com

Few places can be said to be definitively Ithaca, but the local farmers' market is one. Beginning every April, this waterfront temple of ultra-locavorism comes alive in a whirlwind of open-air commerce where folks gather for shopping and eating. The setting is magical, as musicians fiddle, parents push kids in strollers, and Cornell crews practice on the lake. Cuisine ranges from Cuban to Cambodian, exotic to macrobiotic. And what you've heard about Solaz breakfast burritos is true. They're big and everyone eats them. With its eclectic mix of students, activists, artists, families, and professors, the market offers some interesting people-watching.

>*At the east side of downtown Ithaca, take Route 79 heading east.*

SIX MILE CREEK VINEYARD 🍷

1551 Slaterville Road (Route 79), Ithaca, NY 14850
Phone: 607-272-9463
Online: www.sixmilecreek.com

Six Mile Creek is the Finger Lakes oddball. Too far from the winter-moderating protection of Cayuga Lake, Cornell professor Roger Battistella ignored conventional wisdom and bravely planted six acres of white French-hybrid and Vinifera grapes on his patch of land. The extra care he takes to assure the health of the vines helps the plants to withstand temperature extremes, and as a happy consequence, the vineyard's lower yield of fruit results in greater concentration of varietal characters in the wines. For nearly thirty years he has produced a range of wines that confound the experts. Be sure to try the vineyard's flagship wine, appropriately named Ithaca White, a near-dry Cayuga White with a dollop of Chardonnay for a bit of finesse. An aromatic Seyval Blanc resembles Sauvignon Blanc, but Riesling (semi-dry) and Reserve Riesling (dry) steal the show with clean fruit and harmonic acid/sugar balance. Spirits include vodka, gin, grappa, and limoncella.

>*Take Route 79 back to Ithaca, drive across downtown to the West End and pick up Route 89 North along the west shore of Cayuga Lake.*

TAUGHANNOCK FALLS 👀

While it's not exactly in your travel pattern, you shouldn't miss this natural wonder. Take a short drive off Route 89 onto Taughannock Park Road to gawk at New York State's highest waterfall, dropping 215 feet past rocky cliffs that tower nearly 400 feet above the gorge, making it 33 feet taller than Niagara Falls and one of the largest single-drop waterfalls east of the Rocky Mountains. Gorge and rim trails provide spectacular views of the falls from above and below. Visitors in autumn can enjoy the picturesque colors of the surrounding trees. The adjacent park offers hiking and nature trails, camping, picnicking, swimming, fishing, and a boat launch.

BELLWETHER CIDERY 🍷

9070 Route 89, Trumansburg, NY 14886
Phone: (607) 387-9464
Online: www.cidery.com

The wide choice of locally-grown apples gives Bellwether cidermaker Bill Barton a lot to work with, and the results are exceptional varietals and blends. Many of his ciders are concocted from varieties usually considered "eating apples." Empire, Gala, and Fuji are combined in the semi-dry "Original" Hard Cider. "Liberty Spy" has a hearty taste and succulent mouthfeel from the blend of Liberty and Northern Spy apples; the marriage of local Tompkins King and Baldwin produces a tart, refreshing quaff called "King Baldwin." Bellwether's Heritage Hard Cider includes up to 25 varieties of bittersweets and bittersharps (with names like Somerset Redstreak, Tremlett's Bitter, Harry Masters Jersey, and Brown Snout) for a full-bodied drink of rich complexity. Bellwether Wine Cellars, an offshoot of the cidery focuses on Riesling and Pinot Noir made from field- and table-sorted Keuka and Seneca Lake-sourced fruit.

LUCAS VINEYARDS (wine glass icon)

3862 County Road 150 (off Route 89), Interlaken NY, 14847
Phone: (607) 532-4825
Online: www.lucasvineyards.com

The dictionary definition of a family winery, Lucas Vineyards offers a balanced mix of hybrid and vinifera grapes, featuring "museum vines" in the original nursery block. Its star performer is Cayuga White, a local hybrid varietal that once might have defined the region, historically at the heart of the Lucas white wine program. Besides producing a Germanic-style still wine, this early-harvested grape is crafted into the delightful Extra Dry Sparkling Wine. The bustling tasting room offers 15 different wines, including dependable Chardonnay, Gewurztraminer, Cabernet Franc, and consistently excellent Rieslings. The "Tug Boat" series of wines (inspired by family history) are not to be taken too seriously.

SHELDRAKE POINT VINEYARD (wine glass icon)

7448 County Road 153 (off Route 89), Ovid, NY 14521
Phone: (607) 532-9401
Online: www.sheldrakepoint.com

A winery with a good backstory. This remarkable enterprise hugs the shore at Cayuga Lake's deepest point, where the microclimate lengthens the growing season more than two weeks longer than many other areas in the Finger Lakes. After earning a graduate degree from the Cornell Hotel School in 1994, Chuck Tauck joined an adventurous group of people who were intent on converting one of the Point's old dairy farms into a vineyard and winery. That property, resting at the water's edge, is now planted with rows of Riesling, Chardonnay, Gewurztraminer, Pinot Gris, Pinot Noir, Gamay, Merlot, Cabernet Franc, and Cabernet Sauvignon grapes, covering nearly 50 acres. Fantastically rich in fruit flavors, the Sheldrake portfolio of Rieslings dry to semi-dry to ice wine demonstrates that world-class Rieslings have arrived in the Finger Lakes.

HOSMER WINERY

6999 Route 89, Ovid, NY 14521
Phone: (607) 869-3393
Online: www.hosmerwinery.com

Dedicated to the respected European concept of making wine only from his own vineyards, Cameron "Tunker" Hosmer was one of the region's earliest believers in Cabernet Franc as a varietal, and his winery boasts some of the best in the region; softened in French oak barrels for eight to ten months, some say it's one of the finest in America. His vines receive treatment more reminiscent of gardening than viticulture, and it shows, not only in Cab Franc, but in a distinctive Rieslings (from 30 years old vines planted on high-lime Cazenovia loam soils).

THIRSTY OWL WINE COMPANY

6799 Elm Beach Road (off Route 89), Ovid, NY 14521
Phone: (607) 869-5805
Online: www.thirstyowl.com

When Jonathan Cupp purchased a parcel of the former Plane family estate in 2001, he inherited the oldest Riesling vines on Cayuga Lake. Dr. Robert Plane, educator and viticulturalist, planted noble Rieslings on this site in 1972, and after three decades, each drop of wine reflects the character of its grapevine's maturity, so it comes as no surprise that Thirsty Owl bottles regularly capture prestigious medals at wine competitions. Just off the tasting room, the bistro menu offers a range of well-prepared, wine -friendly small plates, salads, flatbreads, and sandwiches.

CAYUGA RIDGE ESTATE WINERY

6800 Route 89, Ovid, NY 14521
Phone: (607) 869-5158
Online: www.cayugaridgewinery.com

Most hybrid grapes were developed by French scientists between 1880 and 1950. Their goal was to combine the finer taste characteristics of European vinifera varieties with the winter-hardiness and disease-resistance of the Native-American varieties. Hybrid varieties continue to be developed specifically for the Finger Lakes and other cool climate regions at Cornell University's New York State Agricultural Experiment Station. The grand old cavernous barn at Cayuga Ridge provides a rustic setting for tasting a range of good to terrific wines, in particular, Cayuga White, a regional hybrid cross, developed at the Experiment Station in 1972. The mother-block of Cayuga White at Cayuga Ridge, blanketing 8 acres of the vineyard with vigorous clusters of greenish-gold, translucent grapes is entrusted to Tom Challen, a skilled grower and winemaker from Canadian wine country. It's an easy-to-enjoy "sipping wine," often compared to Pinot Grigio. Wood-fired pizzas offered from 11:30 AM to 5:30 PM.

KNAPP VINEYARDS ⓨ

2770 County Road 128 (Ernsberger Road) off Route 89, Romulus, NY 14541
Phone: (800) 869-9271
Online: www.knappwine.com

Established by Doug and Suzie Knapp in 1978, the winery was sold to Glenora Wine Cellars in 2000. Both dry and off-dry Rieslings of winemaker Steve DiFrancesco (who also makes the splendid wines at Glenora) are reliable and occasionally superb. Steve's flirtation with Sangiovese may never reach the level of great Tuscan Brunello, but it's worth a sip. Knapp was the first winery on the east coast to operate an Alembic Pot Still for the production of grappa and brandy.

>*Continue on Ernsberger Road; make a right turn onto Route 414.*

SWEDISH HILL WINERY ⓨ

4565 Route 414, Romulus, NY 14541
Phone: (315) 549-8326
Online: www.swedishhill.com

The rustic tasting room is a bit like a country general store, very atmospheric, homey and friendly. Swedish Hill's bullwork with Riesling is one of the reasons why the rest of the world is paying attention. Winemakers Derek Wilbur and Dave Peterson are convinced that blending small amounts of Gewurztraminer to the Dry Riesling and Vignoles to "Blue Waters" (semi-dry) Riesling adds complexity and makes the wines more interesting. Family folklore serves as inspiration for the "Svenska" series of wines, unashamedly driven toward characters of the native varieties.

>*Continue on Route 414 heading north to Seneca Falls. Turn right onto Routes 5e'20.*

AVICOLLI'S PIZZERIA

170 Fall Street (Routes 5&20), Seneca Falls, NY 13148
Phone: (315) 568-2233
Online: www.avicollisrestaurant.com
Corkage Fee: $10

The guy who runs this place missed his calling as a character on *The Sopranos.* Food is standard Italian, but come for the pizza — it's thick, a little chewy, and authentically Neapolitan. The "Romana" is made with fresh-diced tomatoes, garlic, romano and mozzarella cheeses and extra-virgin olive oil. If you're with a group, and some people want pasta, some pizza, and some otherwise, this place will satisfy all comers.

GOULD HOTEL

108 Fall Street (Routes 5&20), Seneca Falls, NY 13148
Phone: (877) 788-4010
Online: www.thegouldhotel.com

The first all-metal pump in the world was cast and assembled in a little stone shop at Green and Ovid Streets in Seneca Falls by Seabury S. Gould's manufacturing company. Goulds Pumps became the world's largest company dedicated to producing only pumps (acquired by ITT Technology in 1997). Construction of the red brick, four-story hotel on Fall Street began in 1919, named the Gould Hotel after its main financier, Norman J. Gould, grandson of the company's founder. The grand old Gould has been revitalized with 48 well-appointed guest rooms.

Sunday

PENNY'S PLACE

2109 Routes 5&20, Seneca Falls, NY 13148
Phone: (315) 568-8746
Breakfast Hours: 6 AM to 1 PM

Walk into this family restaurant, ensconced in the Liberty Plaza strip mall, and it's hard not to feel right at home. Celebrate the simple pleasure of maple syrup atop a stack of pancakes or other well-prepared breakfast fare with homespun style among a cavalcade of characterful customers.

SENECA FALLS

The village is named for the series of small falls and rapids on the Seneca River which drains both Cayuga and Seneca Lakes. Residents claim that when director Frank Capra visited Seneca Falls in 1945, he was inspired to model fictional Bedford Falls in the holiday film classic *It's a Wonderful Life* after their town. Local businessman Norman J. Gould, one of the richest men in town, had great control over politics and economics of the area, much as Henry F. Potter did in the movie. Take a walk across the steel truss bridge over the Cayuga-Seneca Canal, a close match to the bridge that George Bailey jumped from to save Clarence the angel.

>*Follow Routes 5&20 heading west to Waterloo, take Route 96 South to Ovid, then follow Route 96A to Route 414 heading south along the east shore of Seneca Lake (about 30 minutes).*

LAMOREAUX LANDING WINE CELLARS

9224 Route 414, Lodi, NY 14860
Phone: (607) 582-6011
Online: www.lamoreauxwine.com

There are several novel aspects to this enterprise, not the least of which is the striking postmodern winery, designed by architect Bruce Corson and cited by the New York State Chapter of the American Institiute of Architects as one of 60 Notable Projects of the 20th Century. With a spectacular view of the vineyard hillside and lake, it suggests a cross between

Greek Revival architecture, common throughout the Finger Lakes, and one of the region's field barns. One of the most-respected growers in the region, Mark Wagner separates his vineyards into 20 intensely-managed blocks. Site-to-site comparison is interesting among the winery's single-vineyard Rieslings. Taking inspiration from a common practice in the French Loire, his T23 Cabernet Franc is fermented and aged in stainless-steel tanks.

WAGNER VINEYARDS 🍷 🍺

9322 Route 414, Lodi, NY 14860
Phone: (607) 582-6450
Online: www.wagnervineyards.com

If the Finger Lakes were a dartboard, Wagner Vineyards would most likely be its bulls-eye, equidistant from all corners of the region — rather fitting, since this enterprise played a central role in the early growth and development of the region's wine industry. Bill Wagner's vision was to create wines that belong in the company of the great wines of the world. By almost any measure, he succeeded in making that vision a reality. His octagonal building is a Finger Lakes landmark. The winery produces a total of thirty wines, all from the estate's 240 acres of vineyards, and all over the varietal map. Focus is on the award-winning Rieslings — dry, semi-dry, sweet, sparkling, and ice wines (most with practical screw caps). Best of all, the tasting experience here is one of the best educational opportunities in the region. The adjacent microbrewery offers six standard brews in addition to seasonal specialties.

SILVER THREAD VINEYARD 🍷

1401 Caywood Road (off Route 414), Lodi, NY 14860
Phone: (607) 582-6116
Online: www.silverthreadwine.com

Silver Thread falls into the select pilgrimage category. Follow the narrow, unpaved end of Caywood Road heading down toward the lake to one of the smaller, more personal wineries, producing small quantities of Chardonnay, Gewurztraminer, Pinot Noir, and exceptional estate-grown and outsourced single-vineyard Rieslings. Paul Brock (M.S. in Enology and Viticulture from Cornell and former winemaker at Lamoreaux Landing) continues progressive pioneer Richard Figiel's sustainable farming practices and hand-crafted wine production.

DAÑO'S ON SENECA

9564 Route 414, Lodi, NY 14860
Phone: (607) 582-7555
Online: www.danosonseneca.com
Hours: 12 Noon to 9 PM
Corkage Fee: $15

You brush past the chef's herb garden and peer into his kitchen as you enter the restaurant. Daño Hutnik is a superb chef who has played a major role in making the Finger Lakes a food as well as a wine region. The stage of his Austrian wine garden-inspired eatery features sleek counters stacked with pastries and filled with platters of rustic salads and main dishes. Daño's on Seneca is a Finger Lakes translation of the convivial roadside taverns (heurigers) in the wine-growing regions around Vienna. Servers help you assemble a meal to suit your appetite which you can enjoy inside the charming space or on an open-air patio with a view of the lake. Sip the house wine served in glass mugs (viertels) and forget the cares of the world.

SHALESTONE VINEYARDS

9681 Route 414, Lodi, NY 14860
Phone: (607) 582-6600
Online: www.shalestonevineyards.com

Artisan winemaker Rob Thomas has achieved stature in the industry and a loyal following with the mantra, "Red is all we do," a symbol of artistic individualism and a unique niche among the region's producers. From a facility nestled into the hillside, using the earth to keep the temperature constant year round, Rob handcrafts only 10,000 bottles of red wine varietals and creative blends each year, including an interesting Lemberger-Merlot-Syrah proprietary blend cheekily called "Lemberghini." His rich, concentrated beauties are as close as we come to cult wines in the Finger Lakes.

RED NEWT CELLARS

3675 Tichenor Road (just off Route 414), Hector, NY 14841
Phone: (607) 546-4100
Online: www.rednewt.com

One glaring oddity is the fact that Red Newt does not own any vineyards and must purchase all its grapes. However, long-term contracts with dependable growers provide exceptional fruit to confident winemaker David Whiting. The winery produces more than a dozen reds and whites, but its reputation stands on the shoulders of Riesling, the grape that best defines the winery. Best buy is the "Circle" Riesling, a blend of several vineyard plots with fermentation stopped at varying sugar levels, crafted to medium sweetness with vibrant acid providing balance and structure.

BLOOMER CREEK VINEYARDS

5315 Route 414, Hector, NY 14841
Phone: (607) 546-5027
Online: www.bloomercreek.com

The winery takes its name after the rivulet that feeds Cayuga Lake from a spring at the old Bloomer farm. It cuts right through the center of a 10-acre benchland vineyard where Kim Engle practices low-impact farming and manages low crop yields, insuring that each hand-picked cluster of grapes is ripe with intense varietal character. Hard to imagine a more approachable tasting room, housed in a restored Victorian-era carriage house, where well-crafted Pinot Noir, Gamay Noir, Cabernet Franc, and vineyard-designated Rieslings are on display. White wines released under the Tanzen Dame label (homage to the styles of Germany and Alsace) deserve special attention. You might just find the mustachioed Mr. Engle himself pouring your tastings. The people who discover his wines come back vintage after vintage, and that's exactly the idea.

FINGER LAKES DISTILLING

4676 Route 414, Burdett, NY 14818
Phone: (607) 546-5510
Online: www.fingerlakesdistilling.com

The striking micro-distillery stands high above Seneca Lake, housing a custom-built 300-gallon, German-made Holstein pot still for the small-batch distillation of local grapes, including Gewürztraminer, Muscat and Catawba. Among the impressive elixirs is Seneca Drums, a London dry-style gin, energized with eleven botanicals, and McKenzie Rye Whiskey, distilled from New York-grown grain, aged in charred casks and finished in wine barrels from local wineries.

>*Follow Route 414 heading south for one mile, turn left onto Tug Hollow Road (County Road 5), then another left onto Lake Street to the flashing stop light. Continue straight ahead along Route 79 East into Ithaca (about 25 minutes). Once over the Inlet bridge, turn right onto Brindley Street and drive across a one lane bridge to the corner of Taber Street.*

PORTS OF NEW YORK 🍷

815 Taber Street, Ithaca, NY 14850
Phone: (607) 220-6317
Online: www.portsofnewyork.com

Hightail it back to Ithaca for a visit to what is not only the region's most eccentric winery, it's a treasure trove of history. Frédéric Bouché contracts for premium local grapes to make fortified, Port-inspired wines at an enterprise that doubles as a museum of sorts. Frédéric is on hand to pour tastings of his handcrafted wines and tell stories about the vintage winemaking tools he inherited from La Maison Bouché, the winery his family established in Normandy in 1919.

>*Continue on Taber Street, make a right onto Cecil Malone Drive, then another left onto Route 13 heading south. Turn left into Ithaca Shopping Plaza.*

NORTHSIDE WINE & LIQUORS 🛒

222 Elmira Road (off Route 13), Ithaca, NY 14850
Phone: (607) 273-7500
Online: www.northsidewine.com

To supplement bottles you've purchased over the weekend, head over to the local wine supermarket named one of the "50 Best Wine Stores in America" by *Gentlemen's Quarterly*. Since 1959 Northside has provided the greater Ithaca community with an incredible selection of wines from around the world, including bottles that represent nearly all Finger Lakes wineries. Cases of mix-and-match wines net a discount of twenty percent.

>*Take Route 13 heading north; make a right turn onto Clinton Street, and drive across town. Turn left onto Cayuga Street.*

COLTIVARE CULINARY CENTER 🍴

235 South Cayuga Street, Ithaca, NY 14850
Phone: (607) 882-2333
Online: www.coltivareithaca.com
Corkage Fee: $15

Its location at street-level in a municipal parking garage isn't the only thing that sets Coltivare (Italian for "cultivate") apart from other restaurants in the region. This multi-million-dollar facility, including learning labs, demonstration kitchen, wine-tasting room, and restaurant, is the center of Tompkins/Cortland Community College's "Farm-to-Bistro" education program that gives students hands-on experience in every aspect of the food production system. Menus include fresh produce from the TC3 organic farm in Dryden; wine offerings are local and regional.

>*Take Clinton Street (Route 96B) heading east. Follow Route 96B up South Hill and drive a half-mile past Ithaca College.*

LA TOURELLE 🛏

1150 Danby Road (Route 96B), Ithaca, NY 14850
Phone: (800) 765-1492
Online: www.latourelle.com

This lovely retreat is nestled on seventy rolling acres just past Ithaca College atop South Hill. Expertly managed by Scott Wiggins, La Tourelle pampers guests with feather beds in well-appointed rooms. The property includes 4 tennis courts, hiking trails, and spa with a range of services including "vino-therapy" (powdered regional grape seeds rubbed into the skin).

Entry Point:

SKANEATELES

(NORTH - EAST)

WINE TRAILS

DAY TRIP

BLUEWATER GRILL 🍴

11 West Genesse Street (Route 20), Skaneateles, NY 13152
Phone: (315) 685-6600
Hours: Open for breakfast at 8 AM.

Perched on the north shore of Skaneateles Lake, Bluewater offers a full breakfast menu with all the necessities. Ask for a table on the outside deck overlooking the bluish-green waters of the lake and imbibe some local color. Afterwards, head over to nearby Clift Park and onto the long pier that walks out onto the lake.

>Driving west out of the village, turn left onto West Lake Road.

ANYELA'S VINEYARDS 🍷

2433 West Lake Road, Skaneateles, NY 13152
Phone: (315) 685-3797
Online: www.anyelasvineyards.com
Tasting Fee: $2 (10 persons or more $5 per person)

Time to hit the vineyards. Just 5 minutes south of the village, an impressive tasting room reflects the moneyed reputation of Skaneateles and provides a comfortable setting to taste an ambitious range of wines. The style of the Rieslings is one of restraint, not as flamboyantly fruit-driven as some counterparts in the region. The portfolio's strength is with proprietary blends, in which the winemaker adjusts proportions of contributing varietals to the advantages of each year's harvest, i.e. "Overlay," a blend of Cabernet Franc, Pinot Noir, Shiraz and Cabernet Sauvignon.

>Head back to Route 20 and drive west to Seneca Falls (about 30 minutes).

SENECA FALLS 🔭

The village is named for the series of small falls and rapids on the Seneca River which drain both Cayuga and Seneca Lakes. Residents claim that when director Frank Capra visited Seneca Falls in 1945, he was inspired to model fictional Bedford Falls in the holiday film classic *It's a Wonderful Life* after their town. Local businessman Norman J. Gould, one of the richest men in town, had great control over politics and economics of the area, much as Henry F. Potter did in the movie. Take a walk across the

steel truss bridge over the Cayuga-Seneca Canal, a close match to the
bridge that George Bailey jumped from to save Clarence the angel.

>*Follow Routes 5&20 west to Waterloo, take Route 96 south to Ovid, then
Route 414 heading south along the eastern shore of Seneca Lake.*

LAMOREAUX LANDING WINE CELLARS

9224 Route 414, Lodi, NY 14860
Phone: (607) 582-6011
Online: www.lamoreauxwine.com

There are several novel aspects to this enterprise, not the least of which is
the striking postmodern winery, designed by architect Bruce Corson and
built in 1992. With a spectacular view of the vineyard hillside and lake, it
suggests a cross between Greek Revival architecture, common throughout the Finger Lakes, and one of the region's field barns. One of the most-
respected growers in the region, Mark Wagner separates his vineyards
into 20 intensely-managed blocks. Site-to-site comparison is interesting
among the winery's single-vineyard Rieslings. Taking inspiration from a
common practice in the French Loire, his T23 Cabernet Franc is fermented and aged in stainless-steel tanks.

WAGNER VINEYARDS

9322 Route 414, Lodi, NY 14860
Phone: (607) 582-6450
Online: www.wagnervineyards.com

If the Finger Lakes were a dartboard, Wagner Vineyards would most likely be its bulls-eye, equidistant from all corners of the region — rather
fitting, since this enterprise played a central role in the early growth and
development of the region's wine industry. Bill Wagner's vision was to
create wines that belong in the company of the great wines of the world.
By almost any measure, he succeeded in making that vision a reality. His
octagonal building is a Finger Lakes landmark. The winery produces a
total of thirty wines, all from the estate's 240 acres of vineyards, and all
over the varietal map. Focus is on the award-winning Rieslings — dry,
semi-dry, sweet, sparkling, and ice wines (most with practical screw caps).
Best of all, the tasting experience here is one of the best educational opportunities in the region. The adjacent microbrewery offers six standard

brews in addition to seasonal specialties.

DAÑO'S ON SENECA ✪

9564 Route 414, Lodi, NY 14860
Phone: (607) 582-7555
Online: www.danosonseneca.com
Hours: Wednesday thru Monday, 12 Noon to 9 PM
Corkage Fee: $15

You brush past the chef's herb garden and peer into his kitchen as you enter the restaurant. Daño Hutnik is a superb chef who has played a major role in making the Finger Lakes a food as well as a wine region. The stage of his Austrian wine garden-inspired eatery features sleek counters stacked with pastries and filled with platters of rustic salads and main dishes. Dano's on Seneca is a Finger Lakes translation of the convivial roadside taverns (heurigers) in the wine-growing regions around Vienna. Servers help you assemble a meal to suit your appetite which you can enjoy inside the charming space or on an open-air patio with a view of the lake. Sip the house wine served in glass mugs (viertels) and forget the cares of the world.

STANDING STONE VINEYARDS ✪

9934 Route 414, Hector, NY 14841
Phone: (607) 582-6051
Online: www.standingstonewines.com

These are vineyards with a pedigree. First planted by Charles Fournier and Guy DeVeaux of Gold Seal Winery as "Area 13," they represent some of the oldest vinifera plantings in the region. Notable is the North Block Riesling with fruit sourced from the historic vines. Standing Stone (the name inspired by native Indian legend), established in 1991 by Tom and Marti Macinski, has made a name for itself with ice wines. If you have never had the opportunity to try one of these remarkable dessert wines, here's the place to do it.

> *Reverse course and head north on Route 414, then turn left onto Caywood Road.*

SILVER THREAD VINEYARD Ⓨ

1401 Caywood Road (off Route 414), Lodi, NY 14860
Phone: (607) 582-6116
Online: www.silverthreadwine.com

Silver Thread falls into the select pilgrimage category. Follow the narrow, unpaved end of Caywood Road heading down toward the lake to one of the smaller, more personal wineries, producing small quantities of Chardonnay, Gewurztraminer, Pinot Noir, and exceptional estate-grown and outsourced single-vineyard Rieslings. Paul Brock (M.S. in Enology and Viticulture from Cornell and former winemaker at Lamoreaux Landing) continues progressive pioneer Richard Figiel's sustainable farming practices and hand-crafted wine production.

>Go back to Route 414 heading north to Ovid, continue north onto Route 96, then to Routes 5&20 heading east.

MONTEZUMA WINERY Ⓨ

2981 Routes 5&20 East, Seneca Falls, NY 13148
Phone: (315) 568-8190
Online: www.montezumawinery.com

The Martin family translates the fragrant essence of apples, strawberries, blueberries, raspberries, cranberries, peaches, plums, and rhubarb from local farms and orchards into wines that provide a taste of fruit at the peak of the season. A sister operation, Hidden Marsh Distillery, produces liqueurs, vodka, and brandy made with honey, apples, and other seasonal bounty.

>Continue on Routes 5&20 heading east to Auburn. (Routes 5&20 split as you enter the city; continue on Route 20).

MORO'S TABLE Ⓨ

1 East Genesee Street (Route 20), Auburn, NY 13021
Phone: (315) 282-7772
Online: www.morostable.com
Hours: Tuesday thru Saturday, 5 PM to 9 PM
Corkage Fee: $25

Edward Moro earned his stripes in West Coast wine country kitchens before guiding nearby Mirbeau Inn to culinary heights. Now, in his own clubby establishment, the food is stylish and vibrant, a mix of composed salads, sushi and sashimi rolls, and robust main dishes (in full or half portions), each a master work in culinary feng shui. Fine dining here can be spendy but satisfying.

>*Continue on Route 20 heading east to Skaneateles.*

FINGER LAKES LODGING

834 West Genesee Street (Route 20), Skaneateles, NY 13152
Phone: (315) 217-0222
Online: www.fingerlakeslodging.com

Not as luxurious as Mirbeau, its sister property across the street, this former motel has been upgraded with Adirondack flourishes and clean, comfortable rooms. Best bet for an overnight stay, plus you can enjoy the spa amenities at Mirabeau for a small fee without the price of staying there.

Entry Point:

SKANEATELES

(NORTH - EAST)

WINE TRAILS

WEEKEND TOUR

Friday

MIRBEAU INN AND SPA ⊛

851 West Genesee Street (Route 20), Skaneateles, NY 13152
Phone: (315) 685-5006
Online: www.mirbeau.com

Stroll the grounds of this luxury hotel/resort complex, set around a water garden and "Japanese bridge" inspired by impressionist painter Claude Monet's magnificent estate at Giverny, then head over to the Wine Bar for a pre-dinner sampling of small pours from nifty, self-serve, dispensing stations. A menu of small plates is offered for sharing and matching up with the wines. After wetting your whistle, walk next door.

ROSALIE'S CUCINA ⊛

841 West Genesee Street (Route 20), Skaneateles, NY 13152
Phone: (315) 685-2200
Online: www.rosaliescucina.com
Corkage Fee: $20 (limit 2 bottles per table)

This remarkable restaurant is the brainstorm of Auburn native Phil Romano, who earned a national reputation with multi-unit theme eateries including Romano's Macaroni Grill. Rosalie's has the same engaging Italian fare, only it's slightly more upscale and a bit pricier. It's difficult to say what's best about Rosalie's — the bustling, high-energy setting, the well-trained servers, or the terrific food. And for enthusiasts wanting to match local wine to the restaurant's Tuscan cuisine, Rosalie's offers a handful of well-chosen bottles.

FINGER LAKES LODGING ⊛

834 West Genesee Street (Route 20), Skaneateles, NY 13152
Phone: (315) 217-0222
Online: www.fingerlakeslodging.com

Not as luxurious as Mirbeau, its sister property across the street, this former motel has been upgraded with Adirondack flourishes and clean, comfortable rooms. Best bet for an overnight stay, plus you can enjoy the spa amenities at Mirabeau for a small fee without the price of staying there.

Saturday

BLUEWATER GRILL 🍴

11 West Genesse Street (Route 20), Skaneateles, NY 13152
Phone: (315) 685-6600
Hours: Open for breakfast at 8 AM.

Perched on the north shore of Skaneateles Lake, Bluewater offers a full breakfast menu with all the necessities. Ask for a table on the outside deck overlooking the bluish-green waters of the lake and imbibe some local color. Afterwards, head over to nearby Clift Park and onto the long pier that walks out onto the lake.

>Take Route 20 heading west to Seneca Falls, then take Route 414 South.

SWEDISH HILL WINERY 🍷

4565 Route 414, Romulus, NY 14541
Phone: (315) 549-8326
Online: www.swedishhill.com

The rustic tasting room is a bit like a country general store, very atmospheric, homey and friendly. Swedish Hill's bullwork with Riesling is one of the reasons why the rest of the world is paying attention. Winemakers Derek Wilbur and Dave Peterson are convinced that blending small amounts of Gewurztraminer to the Dry Riesling and Vignoles to "Blue Waters" (semi-dry) Riesling adds complexity and makes the wines more interesting. Family folklore serves as inspiration for the "Svenska" series of wines, unashamedly driven toward characters of the native varieties.

>Continue on Route 414 heading south; make a left turn onto Ernsberger Road.

KNAPP VINEYARDS 🍷

2770 County Road 128 (Ernsberger Road), Romulus, NY 14541
Phone: (800) 869-9271

Online: www.knappwine.com

Established by Doug and Suzie Knapp in 1978, the winery was sold to Glenora Wine Cellars in 2000. Both dry and off-dry Rieslings of winemaker Steve DiFrancesco (who also makes the splendid wines at Glenora) are reliable and occasionally superb. Steve's flirtation with Sangiovese may never reach the level of great Tuscan Brunello, but it's worth a sip. Knapp was the first winery on the east coast to operate an Alembic Pot Still for the production of grappa and brandy.

>*Continue on Ernsberger Road; make a right turn onto Route 89 heading south along the western shore of Cayuga Lake.*

CAYUGA RIDGE ESTATE WINERY

6800 Route 89, Ovid, NY 14521
Phone: (607) 869-5158
Online: www.cayugaridgewinery.com

Most hybrid grapes were developed by French scientists between 1880 and 1950. Their goal was to combine the finer taste characteristics of European vinifera varieties with the winter-hardiness and disease-resistance of the Native-American varieties. Hybrid varieties continue to be developed specifically for the Finger Lakes and other cool climate regions by the Cornell University's New York State Agricultural Experiment Station. The grand old cavernous barn at Cayuga Ridge provides a rustic setting for tasting a range of good to terrific wines, in particular, Cayuga White, a regional hybrid cross, developed at the Experiment Station in 1972. The mother-block of Cayuga White at Cayuga Ridge, blanketing 8 acres of the vineyard with vigorous clusters of greenish-gold, translucent grapes is entrusted to Tom Challen, a skilled grower and winemaker from Canadian wine country. It's an easy-to-enjoy "sipping wine," often compared to Pinot Grigio. Wood-fired pizzas offered from 11:30 AM to 5:30 PM.

THIRSTY OWL WINE COMPANY

6799 Elm Beach Road (off Route 89), Ovid, NY 14521
Phone: (607) 869-5805
Online: www.thirstyowl.com

When Jonathan Cupp purchased a parcel of the former Plane family estate in 2001, he inherited the oldest Riesling vines on Cayuga Lake. Dr. Robert Plane, educator and viticulturalist, planted noble Rieslings on this site in 1972, and after three decades, each drop of wine reflects the character of its grapevine's maturity, so it comes as no surprise that Thirsty Owl bottles regularly capture prestigious medals at wine competitions. Just off the tasting room, the bistro menu offers a range of wine-friendly small plates, salads, flatbreads, and sandwiches.

HOSMER WINERY ♟

6999 Route 89, Ovid, NY 14521
Phone: (607) 869-3393
Online: www.hosmerwinery.com

Dedicated to the respected European concept of making wine only from his own vineyards, Cameron "Tunker" Hosmer was one of the region's earliest believers in Cabernet Franc as a varietal, and his winery boasts some of the best in the region; softened in French oak barrels for eight to ten months, some say it's one of the finest in America. His vines receive treatment more reminiscent of gardening than viticulture, and it shows, not only in Cab Franc, but in a distinctive Rieslings (from 30 years old vines planted on high-lime Cazenovia loam soils).

SHELDRAKE POINT VINEYARD ♟

7448 County Road 153 (off Route 89), Ovid, NY 14521
Phone: (607) 532-9401
Online: www.sheldrakepoint.com

A winery with a good backstory. This remarkable enterprise hugs the shore at Cayuga Lake's deepest point, where the microclimate lengthens the growing season up to two weeks longer than many other areas in the Finger Lakes. After earning a graduate degree from the Cornell Hotel School in 1994, Chuck Tauck joined an adventurous group of people who were intent on converting one of the Point's old dairy farms into a vineyard and winery. That property, resting at the water's edge, is now planted with rows of Riesling, Chardonnay, Gewurztraminer, Pinot Gris, Pinot Noir, Gamay, Merlot, Cabernet Franc, and Cabernet Sauvignon grapes, covering nearly 50 acres. Fantastically rich in fruit flavors, the Sheldrake portfolio of Rieslings dry to semi-dry to ice wine demonstrates that world

-class Rieslings have arrived in the Finger Lakes.

LUCAS VINEYARDS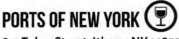

3862 County Road 150 (off Route 89), Interlaken NY, 14847
Phone: (607) 532-4825
Online: www.lucasvineyards.com

The dictionary definition of a family winery, Lucas Vineyards offers a balanced mix of hybrid and vinifera grapes, featuring "museum vines" in the original nursery block. Its star performer is Cayuga White, a local hybrid varietal that once might have defined the region, historically at the heart of the Lucas white wine program. Besides producing a Germanic-style still wine, this early-harvested grape is crafted into the delightful Extra Dry Sparkling Wine. The bustling tasting room offers 15 different wines, including dependable Chardonnay, Gewurztraminer, Cabernet Franc, and consistently excellent Rieslings. The "Tug Boat" series of wines (inspired by family history) are not to be taken too seriously.

>Turn right onto Taughannock Park Road.

TAUGHANNOCK FALLS

Take a short drive off Route 89 onto Taughannock Park Road to view New York State's highest waterfall, dropping 215 feet past rocky cliffs that tower nearly 400 feet above the gorge, making it 33 feet taller than Niagara Falls and one of the largest single-drop waterfalls east of the Rocky Mountains. Gorge and rim trails provide spectacular views of the falls from above and below. Visitors in autumn can enjoy the picturesque colors of the surrounding trees. The adjacent park offers hiking and nature trails, camping, picnicking, swimming, fishing, and a boat launch.

>Continue on Route 89 heading south to Ithaca. Make a right turn onto State Street, then a left onto Brindley Street. Cross the one lane bridge and drive to the corner of Taber Street.

PORTS OF NEW YORK

815 Taber Street, Ithaca, NY 14850
Phone: (607) 220-6317

Online: www.portsofnewyork.com

Welcome to Ithaca and a visit to what is not only the region's most eccentric winery, it's a treasure trove of history. Frédéric Bouché contracts for premium local grapes to make fortified, Port-inspired wines at an enterprise that doubles as a museum of sorts. Frédéric is on hand to pour tastings of his handcrafted wines and tell stories about the vintage winemaking tools he inherited from La Maison Bouché, the winery his family established in Normandy in 1919.

>*Continue on Taber Street, make a left onto Cecil Malone Drive, then another left onto Route 13 heading north. Turn right onto Green Street and drive into downtown.*

JUST A TASTE

116 North Aurora Street, Ithaca, NY 14850
Phone: (607) 277-9463
Online: www.just-a-taste.com
Corkage Fee: $15.

Relax and plan your strategy for tomorrow over dinner at Just a Taste. Working from a kitchen space only slightly larger than a mop closet, chef/owner Jen Irwin and her team create a nightly-changing profusion of locally-inspired tapas and raciones (larger portions of the tapas), so you can eat and share as much or as little as you like without having the formality of a typical dinner. The waitstaff is as accomplished as the cuisine, borderline compulsive when it comes to clearing your table, making room before the next dish arrives. Wine is a passion, and there is passion here aplenty. Sample 45 rotating wines by the glass or "tasting glass" or in flights of five wines, including a dependable "Local Flight." Ah, decisions, decisions.

HILTON GARDEN INN 🛏 🛒

130 E. Seneca Street, Ithaca, NY 14850
Phone: (607) 277-8900
Online: www.hiltongardeninn.com

104 comfortable guestrooms in downtown Ithaca (just around the corner from Just a Taste) each equipped with work desk, high-speed internet

access, microwave and refrigerator. No need to use the in-room coffee-maker, there's a Starbucks at street level. The hotel also provides a down-town home to Sarah's Patisserie, a sweet little gem where French-inspired pastries and chocolates are hand-crafted by owner Tammy Travis, who followed studies at the French Culinary Institute in NYC with a position as pastry assistant to esteemed chocolatier Jacques Torres. It would be a shame to abstain.

Sunday

ITHACA BAKERY

400 North Meadow Street (Route 13 North), Ithaca, NY 14850
Phone: (607) 273-7110
Online: www.ithacabakery.com

Hobnob with the locals at Ithaca Bakery. Turning out 1,000 bagels a day, along with artisan breads and pastries, Ithaca Bakery is also a cafe, deli, and locally-popular gathering place. The self-serve, breakfast buffet bar is exceptional. A glass display case is loaded with salads and side dishes (take along the makings of a picnic at Stewart Park).

>Follow Route 13 heading north and take exit to Route 34 (East Shore Drive). Make a left turn onto Route 34, then an immediate left to the park entrance.

STEWART PARK

Gardner Parkway, Ithaca, NY 14850

On your way out of town, take a side trip (just off Route 34) to the park that hugs the southernmost point of Cayuga Lake, once the site of Wharton Brothers Studio and their production of "cliffhangers" during the silent film era. Today the municipal park provides tennis courts, playground, carousel, duck pond, spray pool, and bird sanctuary.

>Go back to Route 34 (East Shore Drive) heading north. At the traffic light, turn left onto Ridge Road (Route 34B) heading north (about 15 minutes), then turn left onto Center Road. Continue to the intersection of Lake Road.

KING FERRY WINERY (TRELEAVEN WINES)

658 Lake Road, King Ferry, NY 13081
Phone: (315) 364-5100
Online: www.treleavenwines.com

He was known on Capitol Hill as "the gentlemanly gentleman from Massachusetts." After serving three terms as governor and four terms in the U.S. Senate, Leverett Saltonstall stepped down from public service to become a gentleman farmer. His oldest son, also named Leverett, eschewed politics and, instead, distinguished himself in agriculture as professor of agronomy at Cornell, cattle rancher, and seed producer on the 700-acre Treleaven Farm, bordering the eastern shore of Cayuga Lake. On a pasture where beef cattle once roamed, wine grapes now flourish. While the winery surely made its name with big, oak-y Chardonnays, in the last several years Peter and Taci Saltonstall have produced extraordinary, terroir-driven Rieslings, consistently showing well in competitions.

>Turn right onto Lake Road and drive to Route 90 heading north to the village of Aurora.

WELLS COLLEGE

170 Main Street (Route 90), Aurora, NY 13026

Established as a women's college in 1868 by Henry Wells, founder of Wells Fargo and the American Express Company, the school became a co-educational institution in 2005. The campus is situated on 365 beautifully landscaped acres in the small, picturesque village of Aurora, nestled on the shore of beautiful Cayuga Lake.

BET THE FARM WINERY AND GOURMET MARKET

381 Main Street (Route 90), Aurora, NY 13026
Phone: (315) 294-5643
Online: www.betthefarmny.com

While you're in the neighborhood, do as the neighbors do and stop into Bet the Farm. The combination winery tasting room and market operated by Nancy Tisch is the darling of the village of Aurora. Nancy's handmade wines share shelf space with bottles from neighboring wineries, as well as an assortment of flatbreads, dressings, dipping sauces, jams, maple syrups, biscotti, and chocolates from small-scale producers.

AURORA INN

391 Main Street (Route 90), Aurora , NY 13026
Phone: (315) 364-8888
Online: www.aurora-inn.com
Hours: Call for schedule
Corkage Fee: $15.

By the mid-19th century, Aurora was a major stop on the Erie Canal for boats carrying agricultural products from area farmers to New York City. In 1833, Colonel E. B. Morgan, a native of Aurora and original investor in *The New York Times,* built the Aurora Inn, now listed on the National Register of Historic Places. In summer, lunch on the lakeside patio is an idyllic scene right off the pages of a Jane Austen novel. The kitchen takes a bold approach to flavors with an artist's notion of presentation. The wine list includes a thoughtful mix of local red and white varieties that are likely to match up with the food.

MACKENZIE-CHILDS

3260 Route 90, Aurora, NY 13026
Phone: (888) 665-1999
Online: www.mackenzie-childs.com
Hours: 9:30 AM to 6:30 PM

A winding red brick road leads to the home of whimsical, handmade ceramics, enamelware, glassware, furniture, and home accessories. Tour the manufacturing process to observe artisans hand-forming, hand-painting, and hand-trimming each extraordinary piece.

>*Continue on Route 90 heading north to Union Springs.*

HEART & HANDS WINE COMPANY ⊥

4162 Route 90, Union Springs, NY 13160
Phone: (315) 889-8500
Online: www.heartandhandswine.com

Owner/winemaker Tom Higgins is a disciple of Josh Jensen of Calera, a pioneer in the effort to craft Burgundian-style Pinot Noir in America from his limestone-laden soil. It's the presence of limestone clay deposits, heavy with nutrients from marine and shell fossils dating back millions of years ago, that attracted Tom to this specific property. He strives for "true" Pinot Noir through careful placement of vineyard sites and French oak cooperage, and his beautifully-balanced wines are characterized by tremendous energy and bright fruit. Heart & Hands loyalists tend to be such rabid Pinot Noir fans that they sometimes forget that Tom produces very fine Rieslings, as well.

>Continue on Route 90 heading north; take Route 326 (Half Acre Road) to Routes 5&20. Turn right onto Routes 5&20, becoming Route 20 in Auburn, heading east to Skaneateles (about 30 minutes); take a right turn onto West Lake Road.

ANYELA'S VINEYARD 🍷

2433 West Lake Road, Skaneateles, NY 13152
Phone: (315) 685-3797
Online: www.anyelasvineyards.com

Just 5 minutes south of the village, an impressive tasting room reflects the moneyed reputation of Skaneateles and provides a comfortable setting to taste an ambitious range of wines. The style of the Rieslings is one of restraint, not as flamboyantly fruit-driven as some counterparts in the region. The portfolio's strength is with proprietary blends, in which the winemaker adjusts proportions of contributing varietals to the advantages of each year's harvest, i.e. "Overlay," a blend of Cabernet Franc, Pinot Noir, Shiraz and Cabernet Sauvignon.

>Drive back to Route 20 heading west, turn right onto County Line Road, then left onto Center Street Road.

THE RESTAURANT AT ELDERBERRY POND

3978 Center Street Road, Sennett, NY 13021
Phone: (315) 252-3977
Online: www.elderberrypond.com
Hours: 5 PM to 8 PM (March thru December)
Corkage Fee: $12

While many regional restaurants make a special effort to connect with local farms, the Elderberry Pond enterprise is a study in micro-locavorism, completely erasing the line from grower to chef. Based on one of the most diverse organic farms in the Finger Lakes, this is a culinary experience unlike any other. Do not be intimidated by the restaurant's out-of-the-way location on a lonely country road between Skaneateles and Auburn.

>*From the restaurant parking lot, turn right onto Center Street Road, right onto County Line Road, then left onto Route 20 heading east to the village of Skaneateles.*

MIRBEAU INN AND SPA 🛏

851 West Genesee Street (Route 20), Skaneateles, NY 13152
Phone: (315) 685-5006
Online: www.mirbeau.com

Exhausted from a long weekend of driving and wine-tasting? Mirbeau might just be what you need. The style is sublimely relaxed at this luxury hotel/resort complex of six buildings, reminiscent of a French country estate set around Monet-inspired water gardens. Guest rooms include fireplaces, over-sized bathrooms with walk-in showers, soaking tubs, double sinks, and plush mattresses. A full-service spa offers a selection of wraps, massages, facials, and mineral baths. Stroll the Monet-inspired water gardens, then sink into your plush mattress for a good night's sleep.

Entry Point:

CANANDAIGUA

(NORTH - WEST)

BEER TRAILS

DAY TRIP

LAFAYETTE RESTAURANT

408 Lakeshore Drive, Canandaigua, NY 14424
Phone: (585) 394-5383
Online: www.lafayettemotelandrestaurant.com

Breakfast at this 50-year-old local institution is a special pleasure. In a homey, diner-style setting, plates are piled high with eggs, waffles, pancakes, French toast, homemade breads, cinnamon buns, and fat pies. The staff is friendly and service is usually pretty quick. Take home a bag of house-blend coffee beans.

>*Drive west on Lakeshore Drive. Park along the lakefront near the Culinary Center.*

KERSHAW PARK

A bedroom community for nearby Rochester and historically a popular summer retreat for wealthy city folk (Humphrey Bogart's family maintained a summertime cottage on the lake), Canandaigua was built on the site of a Seneca Indian village, becoming an important railroad junction and home port for several steamboats by the mid-19th century. Between 1920 and 1936, old cars among other things were dumped in the lake here to anchor the earth and rocks used to make the park. Stroll along the lakefront walkways or have an impromptu picnic at Kershaw Park, just off Lakeshore Drive, the original shoreline of the lake.

NEW YORK WINE & CULINARY CENTER

800 South Main Street, Canandaigua, NY 14424
Phone: (585) 394-7070
Online: www.nywcc.com

An ideal first stop before you hit the road, this independent, not-for-profit organization serves as Northwest gateway to the culinary bounty of New York State. The Center includes sample tastings of New York State-produced beers (as well as wines). There's also a demonstration theater, hands-on kitchen, gift boutique, exhibit hall, bistro, and outdoor garden.

>*Drive north on Main Street, take a right onto Ontario Street, then another right onto Pleasant Street.*

TWISTED RAIL BREWING COMPANY 🍺

20 Pleasant Street, Canandaigua, NY 14424
Phone: (585) 797-7437
Online: www.twistedrailbrewing.com

They always seem happy to have visitors. This is a "naked brewery" with brewing equipment on full display at the far end of the space, allowing patrons to watch the manufacturing of beers like Cabin Killer IPA among its core lineup, and also special one-offs such as a Wild Hop Ale made with hops picked along the Genesee Valley Greenway Trail near Caledonia. In keeping with its setting in a 100-year-old train depot (shared with the Beehive Brewpub), partners John McMullen, Mike McMullen and Nathan Sirvent have installed tap handles modeled after old railroad spikes and an actual rail that serves as a footrest. Step up to the cherry-wood-topped bar for flights and pints, with 64-ounce growlers-to-go.

>Go back to Main Street heading south towards the lake. Make a left turn onto Routes 5&20 heading east.

NAKED DOVE BREWING 🍺

4048 Routes 5&20, Canandaigua, NY 14424
Phone: (585) 396-2537
Online: www.nakeddovebrewing.com

After earning masterbrewer's credentials at Rohrbach, Custom Brewcafters, and High Falls Brewing, Dave Schlosser set out on his own, building a 15-barrel system and launching Naked Dove Brewing in 2010. While the atmosphere is basic and unassuming, the beers aspire to greater things. Standard offerings, an IPA, porter, amber ale and black raspberry ale, are supplemented with seasonal and specialty brews made with hops sourced from Peterson Farms in Seneca Castle, just eight miles from the brewery. "Expose yourself to Naked Dove" is the motto here, and tap room tasting flights are served in a take-home glass with the brewery logo.

>Continue on Routes 5&20 heading east to Geneva, then turn left onto Castle Street.

LAKE DRUM BREWING 🍺

16 East Castle Street, Geneva, NY 14456
Phone: (315) 789-1200
Online: www.lakedrumbrewing.com

Some believe those distant booms or "drums" over the deep, still waters of Seneca Lake are messages from the Iroquois who once inhabited the area (although scientists explain they are simply the result of geothermal reactions). The legend inspires the name of a nanobrewery start-up, the first operation to produce alcoholic beverages in the city since Prohibition. Victor Pultinas and Jenna LaVita lend their winemaking expertise, fermenting "farmhouse style" brews in red wine barrels with brettanomyces for the sour notes and attractive complexity common in Belgian ales. Beers and house-made ciders are offered by the tasting flights, by the pint, and in growlers-to-go.

OPUS ESPRESSO AND WINE BAR 🍴

486 Exchange Street, Geneva, NY 14456
Phone: (315) 759-5388
Online: www.opusfingerlakes.com
Hours: Monday thru Friday, 7 AM to 4 PM; Saturday, 8 AM to 2 PM

This bouncy, obliging place has a joyfulness to it, offering well-crafted sustenance that speaks to the senses as well as the appetite. A selection of wines by the glass, half-glass, or bottle makes this snug spot popular with nibblers and sippers. Service is expert and agile. If it's grab-and-go you have in mind, a server will fill your hamper with the makings of a first-rate picnic.

> *Return to Routes 5&20 heading west to Route 14, heading south (about 15 minutes). Turn left onto Hansen Point Road.*

CLIMBING BINES 🍺

511 Hansen Point Road (just off Route 14), Penn Yan, NY 14527
Phone: (607) 745-0221
Online: www.climbingbineshopfarm.com

The stars have aligned at Climbing Bines, a hop farm and microbrewery, named for the vining plant that climbs by its shoots and wraps clockwise around its trellis, anchored on a farmstead settled by Chris Hansen's great -grandfather in 1905. Although most breweries don't have the real estate for growing their own ingredients, Chris, along with brewer Brian Karweck have developed a model farm-to-glass enterprise, utilizing 1500 estate-grown hop plants, a mix of 7 varieties, to lend flavors and aromas to a range of brews that are as distinctive and varied as those that grapes and soils give to wine. The "Pandemonium" beers (referencing an old name for Penn Yan in its less civilized past) use other local ingredients — barley, wheat, and rye — grown on nearby Peter Martin farm. The brewery's flagship Imperial IPA, made with earthy Cascade, Chinook and Nugget hops, stays true to the IPA's historical roots. Beers offered by the pint, in a flight, or in take-home growlers.

>*Get back onto Route 14 heading north to Geneva. Take Routes 5&20 heading east, then turn left onto Castle Street.*

RED DOVE TAVERN

30 Castle Street, Geneva, NY 14456
Phone: (315) 781-2020
Online: www.reddovetavern.com
Dinner Hours: 4 PM to 10 PM (Tuesday thru Saturday)
Corkage Fee: $15

Its name an homage to Arthur Dove, the American modernist painter raised in Geneva, this friendly, downtown "gastropub" offers local and seasonally-inspired small plates and entrees from a frequently changing chalkboard menu, a selection of microbrews, and Finger Lakes wines "on tap" by the glass, half carafe, or full carafe.

>*Take Castle Street back out to Routes 5&20.*

RAMADA GENEVA LAKEFRONT

41 Lake Front Drive, Geneva, NY 14456
Phone: (315) 789-0400
Online: www.genevaramada.com

Overlooking the Seneca Lake waterfront, all 148 (mostly non-smoking) rooms have 50-channel cable TV, wireless high speed internet, in-room safe, microwave, coffee maker, and a mini-fridge for the beer you purchased earlier in the day. The beach at Seneca Lake State Park is only two miles away, or you can take a dip in the heated indoor pool.

Entry Point:

CANANDAIGUA

(NORTH - WEST)

BEER TRAILS

WEEKEND TOUR

Friday

RHEINBLICK GERMAN RESTAURANT 🍴

224 South Main Street, Canandaigua, NY 14424
Phone: (585) 905-0950
Online: www.rheinblick.hostei.com
Corkage Fee: none

The first wave of German immigrants arrived in Western New York in the mid-1800s, growing hops and honing beer brewing to a fine art. Dinner in the cozy dining room or at a table in the adjacent alley includes an impressive selection of German beers, both draft and bottled, to accompany schnitzels, wursts, bratens, and other pork, veal, and chicken entrées, along with starters and traditional sides like sauerkraut, egg noodles, and spätzle.

>*Drive north on Main Street, take a right onto Ontario Street, then another right onto Pleasant Street.*

BEE HIVE BREW PUB 🍺

20 Pleasant Street, Canandaigua, NY 14424
Phone: (585) 919-2471
Online: www.beehivebrewpub.com

Discerning beer drinkers find their way to the Bee Hive. If you're up for a late-night pint, this beer bar has 32 brews on draft, including craft beers made by next-door-neighbor Twisted Rail Brewing specifically for the pub.

>*Go back to Main Street heading south towards the lake.*

THE INN ON THE LAKE 🛏

770 South Main Street, Canandaigua, NY 14424
Phone: (800) 228-2801
Online: www.theinnonthelake.com

Perched at the edge of Canandaigua Lake's north shore, just a few steps from the Wine & Culinary Center. Request a room with lakefront patio or balcony, and bring a bathing suit for the indoor or outdoor pool. Good selection of local beers at either The Lounge or The Sand Bar, the seasonal poolside bar.

Saturday

LAFAYETTE RESTAURANT

408 Lakeshore Drive, Canandaigua, NY 14424
Phone: (585) 394-5383
Online: www.lafayettemotelandrestaurant.com

Breakfast at this 50-year-old local institution is a special pleasure. In a homey, diner-style setting, plates are piled high with eggs, waffles, pancakes, French toast, homemade breads, cinnamon buns, and fat pies. The staff is friendly and service is usually pretty quick. Take home a bag of house-blend coffee beans.

>Drive west on Lakeshore Drive. Park along the lakefront near the Culinary Center.

KERSHAW PARK

A bedroom community for nearby Rochester and historically a popular summer retreat for wealthy city folk (Humphrey Bogart's family maintained a summertime cottage on the lake), Canandaigua was built on the site of a Seneca Indian village, becoming an important railroad junction and home port for several steamboats by the mid-19th century. Between 1920 and 1936, old cars among other things were dumped in the lake here to anchor the earth and rocks used to make the park. Stroll along the lakefront walkways or have an impromptu picnic at Kershaw Park, just off Lakeshore Drive, the original shoreline of the lake.

NEW YORK WINE & CULINARY CENTER

800 South Main Street, Canandaigua, NY 14424
Phone: (585) 394-7070

Online: www.nywcc.com

An ideal first stop before you hit the road, this independent, not-for-profit organization serves as Northwest gateway to the culinary bounty of New York State. The Center includes sample tastings of New York State-produced beers (as well as wines). There's also a demonstration theater, hands-on kitchen, gift boutique, bistro, and outdoor garden.

>Drive north on Main Street, take a right onto Ontario Street, then another right onto Pleasant Street.

TWISTED RAIL BREWING COMPANY 🍺

20 Pleasant Street, Canandaigua, NY 14424
Phone: (585) 797-7437
Online: www.twistedrailbrewing.com

They always seem happy to have visitors. This is a "naked brewery" with brewing equipment on full display at the far end of the space, allowing patrons to watch the manufacturing of beers like Cabin Killer IPA among its core lineup, and also special one-offs such as a Wild Hop Ale made with hops picked along the Genesee Valley Greenway Trail near Caledonia. In keeping with its setting in a 100-year-old train depot (shared with the Beehive Brewpub), partners John McMullen, Mike McMullen and Nathan Sirvent have installed tap handles modeled after old railroad spikes and an actual rail that serves as a footrest. Step up to the cherrywood-topped bar for flights and pints, with 64-ounce growlers-to-go.

>Go back to Main Street heading south towards the lake. Make a left turn onto Routes 5&20 heading east.

NAKED DOVE BREWING 🍺

4048 Routes 5&20, Canandaigua, NY 14424
Phone: (585) 396-2537
Online: www.nakeddovebrewing.com

After earning masterbrewer's credentials at Rohrbach, Custom Brew-cafters, and High Falls Brewing, Dave Schlosser set out on his own, building a 15-barrel system and launching Naked Dove Brewing in 2010.

While the atmosphere is basic and unassuming, the beers aspire to greater things. Standard offerings, an IPA, porter, amber ale and black raspberry ale, are supplemented with seasonal and specialty brews made with hops sourced from Peterson Farms in Seneca Castle, just eight miles from the brewery. "Expose yourself to Naked Dove" is the motto here, and tap room tasting flights are served in a take-home glass with the brewery logo.

>*Continue on Routes 5&20 heading east to Geneva. Make a left turn onto Castle Street.*

OPUS ESPRESSO AND WINE BAR 🍴

486 Exchange Street, Geneva, NY 14456
Phone: (315) 759-5388
Online: www.opusfingerlakes.com
Hours: Saturday, 8 AM to 2 PM

This bouncy, obliging place has a joyfulness to it, offering well-crafted sustenance that speaks to the senses as well as the appetite. A selection of wines by the glass, half-glass, or bottle makes this snug spot popular with nibblers and sippers. Service is expert and agile. If it's grab-and-go you have in mind, a server will fill your hamper with the makings of a first-rate picnic.

>*Return to Routes 5&20 heading west to Route 14, heading south (about 15 minutes). Turn left onto Hansen Point Road.*

CLIMBING BINES 🍺

511 Hansen Point Road (just off Route 14), Penn Yan, NY 14527
Phone: (607) 745-0221
Online: www.climbingbineshopfarm.com

The stars have aligned at Climbing Bines, a hop farm and microbrewery, named for the vining plant that climbs by its shoots and wraps clockwise around its trellis, anchored on a farmstead settled by Chris Hansen's great-grandfather in 1905. Although most breweries don't have the real estate for growing their own ingredients, Chris, along with brewer Brian Karweck have developed a model farm-to-glass enterprise, utilizing 1500 estate-grown hop plants, a mix of 7 varieties, to lend flavors and aromas to a range of brews that are as distinctive and varied as those that grapes and soils give to wine. The "Pandemonium" beers (referencing an old name for Penn Yan in its less civilized past) use other local ingredients — barley, wheat, and rye — grown on nearby Peter Martin farm. The brewery's flagship Imperial IPA, made with earthy Cascade, Chinook and Nugget hops, stays true to the IPA's historical roots. Beers offered by the pint, in a flight, or in take-home growlers.

>*Return to Route 14 heading south.*

MILES CRAFT ALES AT MILES WINE CELLARS

168 Randall Crossing Road (off Route 14), Himrod, NY 14842
Phone: (607) 243-7742
Online: www.mileswinecellars.com

It's neither a winery nor a brewery, but this 200-year-old Greek Revival home, steeped in history, is one of the most scenic places to taste both local wine and beer. As an experienced and respected grower, Doug Miles devotes full time to the grapevines and relinquishes winemaking to Peter Bell at nearby Fox Run. Besides a sip or two of the wines, sample the small-batch ales made at the Abandon Brewing facility in Penn Yan, then stroll the surrounding waterfront grounds.

>*Get back onto Route 14 heading south and drive to Dundee.*

STARKEY'S LOOKOUT

5428 New York 14, Dundee, NY 14837
Phone: (607) 678-4043
Online: www.starkeyslookout.com

Don't look for a hop farm or vineyard here, or for that matter, any brewing or winemaking facilities. A doctor and a lawyer partnered to build this mammoth tasting room — the size of a major hotel lobby — for contracted beers and wines. The beers are produced in the public market district of Rochester by the Rohrbach Brewing Company. Worth the stop to pick up a couple of 750-ml bottles of full-bodied Scotch Ale (the name given to a strong 19th century-style Edinburgh pale ale) with malty sweetness and 8.4% alcohol.

>*Continue on Route 14 heading south to the village of Watkins Glen.*

CROOKED ROOSTER BREWPUB

223-301 North Franklin Street (Route 14), Watkins Glen, NY 14891
Phone: (607) 535-9797
Online: www.roosterfishbrewing.com
Hours: 11:30 AM to 9 PM
Corkage Fee: $10

The drinking wing of the Wildflower Café is a chummy brewpub offering "Dark Nut Brown Ale" and "Dog Tooth Pale Ale" among a dozen brews made with organic ingredients and Seneca Lake water. Ambitious pub fare includes Buffalo wings, barbeque ribs, burgers and sausages, local organic steak, and pizza toppings on hand-stretched brewer's malt dough.

>*Continue on North Franklin Street (Route 14) heading south across the village. Just past the park entrance, make a right turn onto Route 329 (Old Corning Road), then another right onto Walnut Road.*

SENECA LODGE

3600 Walnut Road, Watkins Glen, NY 14891
Phone: (607) 535-2014
Online: www.senecalodge.com

Swing open the wide, creaking door and walk through a wood-paneled dining room. Pull up a stool at one of the most unusual bars you will ever see. Since 1948, the Seneca Lodge Tavern Room has been a gathering place for the drivers and crews of the Grand Prix races. Behind the bar, laurel wreaths from the Formula 1 races of the 1970s hang from hundreds of arrows shot into the wall by archers who frequent the lodge for archery championships. Suspended from the ceiling are tires from NASCAR champions. House-brewed beers on tap include Blonde Ale, Belgian-style, and an agressively-hopped IPA. This is a place to drink beer, not just taste it.

>*Drive back to North Franklin Street (Route 14); turn left, heading north.*

WATKINS GLEN HARBOR HOTEL 🛏️

16 North Franklin Street (Route 14), Watkins Glen, NY 14891
Phone: (607) 535-6116
Online: www.watkinsglenharborhotel.com

Nesting on the Southern-most point of Seneca Lake, hotel guestrooms are appointed with comfy pillow-topped mattresses covered with 310-thread count linens, plush duvet covers and feather pillows. Request a room with a view of the lake and enjoy a glass of local brew on your balcony.

Sunday

BLUE POINTE GRILLE 🍴

16 North Franklin Street (Route 14), Watkins Glen, NY 14891
Phone: (607) 535-6116
Online: www.watkinsglenharborhotel.com

Start off your day with above-average hotel dining room breakfast fare, including omelets, made-to-order eggs, steak & eggs, cereals, waffles, French toast, pancakes, and coffee or espresso. Ask for a table on the lakeside patio and enjoy breakfast al fresco overlooking Seneca harbor.

WATKINS GLEN STATE PARK

You loved those pancakes. Now walk them off at the most famous of the Finger Lakes State Parks, with a reputation for leaving visitors spellbound. Within two miles, the glen's stream descends 400 feet past 200-foot cliffs, generating 19 waterfalls along its course. In 1933 President Franklin Roosevelt created the Civilian Conservation Corps in an effort to put unemployed men to work. They were responsible for building many of the present day pathways winding over and under waterfalls and through the spray of Cavern Cascade. The tunnels in the gorge were hand-cut in the rock. Wear comfortable shoes.

>Beginning at the corner North Franklin Street (Route 14) and 4th Street (Route 414), follow Route 414 north along the eastern shore of Seneca Lake.

TWO GOATS BREWING

5027 Route 414, Hector, NY 14818
Phone: (607) 546-2337
Online: www.twogoatsbrewing.com

This converted barn, just off the Seneca Lake wine trail, has a dive bar vibe without being a dive. No formal tastings here, just do as the locals do — belly up to the bar for an interesting range of house-brewed beers (as well as other beers on tap and even more in bottles), munch fresh-popped popcorn, and shoot darts. The best place to sip is on the wrap-around porch with a spectacular view of the lake and surrounding vineyards.

>*Continue on Route 414 heading north.*

WAGNER VALLEY BREWERY

9322 Route 414, Lodi, NY 14860
Phone: (607) 582-6450
Online: www.wagnerbrewing.com

The winery produces a total of thirty wines, all from the estate's 240 acres of vineyards, and all over the varietal map, but wine is not the only intriguing product offered here. The brew system at Wagner's is an imported 20-barrel, steam fired, four-vessel, German-style brewhouse, following the German Purity Law (or Reinheitsgebot), using only malt, hops, yeast, and water to make beer. Offering four standards and a half-dozen seasonal brews. Mainstays include "Sled Dog Doppelbock," an expressive, russet-hued tan-headed, Bavarian-style double bock, light and amber lagers, and an IPA, all available in 12-ounce bottles. Head next door to the Ginny Lee Café for lunch overlooking the vineyards; feast on soups, salads, sandwiches, and flatbreads.

>*Follow Route 414 to Route 96A. In Ovid, Routes 414 & 96A split; turn left and continue on Route 96A, then make a left onto Lerch Road.*

WAR HORSE BREWING COMPANY
AT THREE BROTHERS WINERY

623 Lerch Road, Geneva, NY 14456

Phone: (315) 585-4432
Online: www.3brotherswinery.com/war-horse

The Three Brothers venture is more like an amusement park than a winery or brewery. It's rustic, quaint, and all about entertainment. If fact, while they do grow grapes and make wines, the "War Horse Brewing Company" is not a brewery at all, but a sales room for beers produced by CB Craft Brewers in Honeoye Falls. If you can weave your way past the crowds at the wine slushie stand, sample offerings including the Riesling Ale — an Americanized version of a Hefeweizen spiked with Riesling grape juice. It's a refreshing tipple when served with a lemon wedge. Available by the growler or 22-ounce bottles.

>*Get back onto Route 96A heading north to Geneva. Make a left turn onto Routes 5&20, then a right onto Castle Street.*

LAKE DRUM BREWING 🍺

16 East Castle Street, Geneva, NY 14456
Phone: (315) 789-1200
Online: www.lakedrumbrewing.com

Some believe those distant booms or "drums" over the deep, still waters of Seneca Lake are messages from the Iroquois who once inhabited the area (although scientists explain they are simply the result of geothermal reactions). The legend inspires the name of a nanobrewery start-up, the first operation to produce alcoholic beverages in the city since Prohibition. Victor Pultinas and Jenna LaVita lend their winemaking expertise, fermenting "farmhouse style" brews in red wine barrels with brettanomyces for the sour notes and attractive complexity common in Belgian ales. Beers and house-made ciders are offered by the tasting flights, by the pint, and in growlers-to-go.

BELHURST CASTLE 🍴 🛏

4069 Route 14 South, Geneva, NY 14456
Phone: (315) 781-0201
Online: www.belhurst.com
Dinner Hours: 5 PM to 9:30 PM

In 1885, Carrie Harron Collins, a wealthy descendant of Henry Clay of

Kentucky, hired an architect and a crew of fifty laborers to begin work on a fairy-tale castle set amid twenty acres of forest on the shore of Seneca Lake. Four years later, Belhurst, the three-story, turreted, red-stone curiosity, was completed. The historic castle's gorgeous, over-the-top interior is an appropriate setting for Edgar's, not for the faint of heart when it comes to pushing carnivorous limits. The menu features Flat Iron, Porterhouse, and New York Strip Steaks, Filet Mignon, Roast Prime Ribs of Beef, Veal, Lamb, and Pork entrees. The sprawling Belhurst complex now includes two hotels. You can stay in the original castle chambers or the adjacent Vinifera Inn with king-size beds, Jacuzzis, gas fireplaces, and two -person showers. Listed on the National Register of Historic Places.

Entry Point:

HAMMONDSPORT

(SOUTH - WEST)

BEER TRAILS

DAY TRIP

KEUKA ARTISAN BAKERY & DELI

49 Shethar Street, Hammondsport, NY 14840
Phone: (607) 224-4001
Online: www.keukaartisanbakery.com
Breakfast Hours: 7 AM to 11 AM

Just steps from the village square, the aroma of fresh-baked breads and sweets will stop you in your tracks. The breads enclose breakfast sandwiches and are toasted to accompany omelets-of-the-day. Save room for dessert from the pastry counter with locally-roasted coffee or espresso, and don't forget to take along a warm-out-of-the-oven baguette to support your day of beer tasting.

PULTENEY SQUARE

Picturesque Hammondsport, on the South end of the lake, has a long history as a vintner's enclave. The first wine grapes in the Finger Lakes were cultivated here in 1829 by William Bostwick, minister of St. James Episcopal Church, and commercial wine production began here in 1860. Many of the fine homes along Lake Street were built by winery owners and winemakers during the second half of the 19th century. Take a stroll around the village square of "the Coolest Small Town in America," according to *Budget Travel Magazine.*

>*Take Main Street (Route 54A) south out of town. Turn right onto Route 54 heading west.*

GLENN H. CURTISS AVIATION MUSEUM

8419 Route 54, Hammondsport, NY 14840
Phone: (607) 569-2160
Online: www.glennhcurtissmuseum.org

Since the breweries don't open until noon, this is your opportunity for a glimpse into local aviation history, and not entirely off topic — the legendary Glenn Curtiss was an avid beer drinker, often seen wiping the foam off his thick mustache. He made innumerable contributions to early aviation, producing and selling the first private airplane, receiving pilot's license #1, design and construction of the first successful pontoon aircraft in America, invention of dual pilot control, and design of retractable landing gear. The museum houses a collection of Curtiss' airplanes and motorcycles, as well as displays, exhibits, and interactive gallery relating to local winemaking and turn of-the-century life. (Admission: Adults $8.50; Seniors $7; Students $5.50; Kids free)

>*Get back onto Route 54 heading east.*

FINGER LAKES BEER COMPANY 🍺

8462 Route 54, Hammondsport, NY 14840
Phone: (607) 569-3311
Online: www.fingerlakesbeercompany.com

Sometimes going against the grain is a good thing. In 2010, amateur brewers and avid craft beer enthusiasts Wayne Peworchik and Mark Goodwin established this microbrewery smack dab in what has always been known as wine country. Yet both locals and tourists have proved equally gregarious beer drinkers, keeping the tap room hopping, as the range of offerings evolves and becomes more sophisticated. Sample year-round standbys Copper Ale and Hammonds-Porter (brewed with chocolate malt and vanilla beans), and seasonal wheat beer brewed with fresh watermelon. All beers travel in growlers or bottles.

>*Turn left onto 54A heading north out of the village, then bear left onto G. H. Taylor Memorial Drive.*

BULLY HILL VINEYARDS

8843 G. H. Taylor Memorial Drive, Hammondsport, NY 14840
Phone: (607) 868-3610
Online: www.bullyhill.com

Bully Hill's founder, Walter Taylor, was a larger-than-life character in a sweeping epic of Finger Lakes Wine Country. The grandson of the founder of the Taylor Wine Company and an eager provocateur, Walter railed against the "wine factory" the company had become by the time it was swallowed up by Coca-Cola in 1977. He was a marketing genius whose sense of humor provided an antidote to wine snobbery. While the rascally, holy-terror personality of Walter Taylor is gone from his beloved winery, his anti-establishment wine making and off-the-wall labels have earned him a hero's status in the Finger Lakes. Visit here, soak up a bit of the lore of the legendary "Baron of Bully Hill," and stay for lunch at the restaurant. Local craft beers on tap accompany small plates, burgers, sandwiches, and smoked chicken wings by the dozen or half-dozen.

>*Take Sanford Road to Route 76. Turn left, heading north (about 10 minutes); turn left onto Briglin Road.*

KEUKA BREWING COMPANY

8572 Briglin Road, Hammondsport, NY 14840
Phone: (607) 868-4648
Online: www.keukabrewingcompany.com

Sequestered among hills along the wine trail, the tasting room here is not the kind of place where you want to spend hours chatting with old friends, but who cares? It's all about the beer. This back lane brewery, founded in 2008 by Richard and Linda Musso who put son Mark in charge of the 10-barrel brewhouse. The Mussos have found a strong following for a range of craft beers including Briglin Road Red, Bluff Point Porter and Hoppy Laker IPA. In 2014, Keuka Brewing won the F. X. Matt Cup at the TAP New York Craft Beer Festival as the "Best Craft Brewery" in the state.

>*Get back onto Route 76; continue heading north to the intersection of Judson Road.*

STEUBEN BREWING COMPANY

10286 Judson Road, Hammondsport, NY 14840
Phone: (607) 332-3000
Online: www.steubenbrewingcompany.com

Microbrew pilgrims will enjoy this new outpost, overlooking Keuka Lake's bluff at the northern edge of a county named in honor of Baron von Steuben, a German general who fought on the American side during the Revolutionary War. With beer so often being the beverage of choice among people who work in the wine industry, a brewery smack dab in the middle of wine country came naturally to the Zimar family, headed by Jim Zimar, the winemaker at Prejean Winery. Sons Chad and Rick take charge of a seven-barrel system, turning out ales and lagers in 200-gallon batches. In addition, a single-barrel pilot system produces 30-gallon supply for seasonals and experimentals, including an unfiltered cask-conditioned ale which goes through secondary fermentation. Sample fresh brews by the flight, half-pint or pint, and get a growler to go.

>*Reverse course, heading south to the village of Hammondsport.*

THE VILLAGE TAVERN (🍴)

30 Mechanic Street, Hammondsport, NY 14840
Phone: (607) 569-2528
Online: www.villagetaverninn.com
Hours: Daily, 5 PM to 9 PM (Memorial Day to October 31); Call for off-season schedule
Corkage Policy: No outside wine allowed

Winery folks have made the Village Tavern their central gathering place, but anyone feels welcome. Careful not to drop the wine list on your foot, as you could really hurt yourself. One of the thrills of eating here is the opportunity to browse through the encyclopedic, all-Finger Lakes wine list, novel for both its breadth and entertainment value. The Tavern also takes its beers very seriously with a range of good crafts, including the local micros. Eclectic dinner menu offers something for everyone.

KEUKA LAKESIDE INN (🛏️)

24 Water Street, Hammondsport, NY 14840
Phone: (607) 569-2600
Online: www.keukalakesideinn.com

It's all about the view at this updated, old-style motel perched at the water's edge and just a short walk from the village square. At the end of the day, relax in the gazebo and contemplate the serene waters of Keuka, the name the Seneca people gave to the lake for their "canoe landing."

Entry Point:

HAMMONDSPORT

(SOUTH - WEST)

BEER TRAILS

WEEKEND TOUR

Friday

THE VILLAGE TAVERN 🍴

30 Mechanic Street, Hammondsport, NY 14840
Phone: (607) 569-2528
Online: www.villagetaverninn.com
Hours: 5 PM to 9 PM
Corkage Policy: No outside wine allowed

Winery folks have made the Village Tavern their central gathering place, but anyone feels welcome. Careful not to drop the wine list on your foot, as you could really hurt yourself. One of the thrills of eating here is the opportunity to browse through the encyclopedic, all-Finger Lakes wine list, novel for both its breadth and entertainment value. The Tavern also takes its beers very seriously with a range of good crafts, including the local micros. Eclectic dinner menu offers something for everyone.

KEUKA LAKESIDE INN 🛏

24 Water Street, Hammondsport, NY 14840
Phone: (607) 569-2600
Online: www.keukalakesideinn.com

It's all about the view at this updated, old-style motel perched at the water's edge and just a short walk from the village square. At the end of the day, relax in the gazebo and contemplate the serene waters of Keuka, the name the Seneca people gave to the lake for their "canoe landing."

Saturday

KEUKA ARTISAN BAKERY & DELI 🍴

49 Shethar Street, Hammondsport, NY 14840
Phone: (607) 224-4001
Online: www.keukaartisanbakery.com
Breakfast Hours: 7 AM to 11 AM

Just steps from the village square, the aroma of fresh-baked breads and sweets will stop you in your tracks. The breads enclose breakfast sandwiches and are toasted to accompany omelets-of-the-day. Save room for dessert from the pastry counter with locally-roasted coffee or espresso, and don't forget to take along a warm-out-of-the-oven baguette to support your day of beer tasting.

PULTENEY SQUARE 🔭

Picturesque Hammondsport, on the South end of the lake, has a long history as a vintner's enclave. The first wine grapes in the Finger Lakes were cultivated here in 1829 by William Bostwick, minister of St. James Episcopal Church, and commercial wine production began here in 1860. Many of the fine homes along Lake Street were built by winery owners and winemakers during the second half of the 19th century. Take a stroll around the village square of "the Coolest Small Town in America," according to *Budget Travel Magazine*.

>*Take Main Street (Route 54A) south out of town. Turn right onto Route 54 heading west.*

GLENN H. CURTISS AVIATION MUSEUM 🔭

8419 Route 54, Hammondsport, NY 14840
Phone: (607) 569-2160
Online: www.glennhcurtissmuseum.org

Since the breweries don't open until noon, this is your opportunity for a glimpse into local aviation history, and not entirely off topic — the legendary Glenn Curtiss was an avid beer drinker, often seen wiping the foam off his thick mustache. He made innumerable contributions to early aviation, producing and selling the first private airplane, receiving pilot's license #1, design and construction of the first successful pontoon aircraft in America, invention of dual pilot control, and design of retractable landing gear. The museum houses a collection of Curtiss' airplanes and motorcycles, as well as displays, exhibits, and interactive gallery relating to local winemaking and turn of-the-century life. (Admission: Adults $8.50; Seniors $7; Students $5.50; Kids free)

>*Get back onto Route 54 heading east.*

FINGER LAKES BEER COMPANY 🍺

8462 New York 54, Hammondsport, NY 14840
Phone: (607) 569-3311
Online: www.fingerlakesbeercompany.com

Sometimes going against the grain is a good thing. In 2010, amateur brewers and avid craft beer enthusiasts Wayne Peworchik and Mark Goodwin established this microbrewery smack dab in what has always been known as wine country. Yet both locals and tourists have proved equally gregarious beer drinkers, keeping the tap room hopping, as the range of offerings evolves and becomes more sophisticated. Sample year-round standbys Copper Ale and Hammonds-Porter (brewed with chocolate malt and vanilla beans), and seasonal wheat beer brewed with fresh watermelon. All beers travel in growlers or bottles.

>*Continue on Route 54 heading east; turn left onto 54A heading north out of the village, then bear left onto Route 76, heading north (about 10 minutes); turn left onto Briglin Road.*

KEUKA BREWING COMPANY 🍺

8572 Briglin Road, Hammondsport, NY 14840
Phone: (607) 868-4648
Online: www.keukabrewingcompany.com

Sequestered among hills along the wine trail, the tasting room here is not the kind of place where you want to spend hours chatting with old friends, but who cares? It's all about the beer. This back lane brewery was founded in 2008 by Richard and Linda Musso who put son Mark in charge of the 10-barrel brewhouse. The Mussos have found a strong following for a range of craft beers including Briglin Road Red, Bluff Point Porter and Hoppy Laker IPA. In 2014, Keuka Brewing won the F. X. Matt Cup at the TAP New York Craft Beer Festival as the "Best Craft Brewery" in the state.

>*Get back onto Route 76; continue heading north to the intersection of Judson Road.*

STEUBEN BREWING COMPANY 🍺

10286 Judson Road, Hammondsport, NY 14840
Phone: (607) 332-3000
Online: www.steubenbrewingcompany.com

Microbrew pilgrims will enjoy this new outpost, overlooking Keuka Lake's bluff at the northern edge of a county named in honor of Baron von Steuben, a German general who fought on the American side during the Revolutionary War. With beer so often being the beverage of choice among people who work in the wine industry, a brewery smack dab in the middle of wine country came naturally to the Zimar family, headed by Jim Zimar, the winemaker at Prejean Winery. Sons Chad and Rick take charge of a seven-barrel system, turning out ales and lagers in 200-gallon batches. In addition, a single-barrel pilot system produces 30-gallon batches for seasonals and experimentals, including an unfiltered cask-conditioned ale which goes through secondary fermentation. Sample fresh brews by the flight, half-pint or pint for growlers to go.

>*Continue on Judson Road (Route 74) heading north; turn right onto Rolf Hill Road, then left onto Route 54A heading north along the western shore of Keuka Lake. At the Branchport intersection, turn right and continue of Route 54A.*

ESPERANZA MANSION 🍴

3456 Route 54A, Bluff Point, NY 14478
Phone: (315) 536-4400
Online: www.esperanzamansion.com
Hours: Call for seasonal schedule
Corkage Fee: $15

John Nicholas Rose, the son of Robert and Jane Rose, journeyed to the Finger Lakes from the family plantation in Stafford County, Virginia. He purchased 1,000 acres of land and completed construction of the home he called "Esperanza" (derived from the Latin word for "hope") in 1838. It's a little piece of heaven sitting astride the Keuka highlands — a Greek Revival mansion lovingly restored to its 19th century splendor. Offering three separate dining areas, outdoor terrace and patio seating with a breathtaking view. Put on your sunglasses and grab an outdoor seat. Among the dazzling vistas along Keuka Lake, this place may be the best.

>*Continue on Route 54A heading north. Turn left onto Merritt Hill Road.*

ABANDON BREWING COMPANY 🍺

2994 Merritt Hill Road, Penn Yan, NY 14527
Phone: (585) 209-3276
Online: www.abandonbrewing.com

Sheltered in a restored nineteenth-century barn amidst seven acres of vineyards, apple orchards, walnut groves, and a hopyard with six varieties to flavor their beers, this farmhouse brewery is simply a spectacular place to visit, one of the region's charming pastoral retreats. The helpful staff receives brew pilgrims with open arms. Partner and brewmaster Jeff Hillebrandt interned at Custom Brewcrafters, studied brewing at schools in Chicago and Munich, Germany, then worked for Belgian beer specialist Brewery Ommegang before joining the team at Abandon. The mastery of his profession is on display in a range of undeniably eclectic offerings, many crafted with crops that grow on and around Abandon Acres, including walnuts and black currants. After sampling at the tasting bar, take a pint of your favorite out on the deck overlooking Keuka Lake from the top of Merritt Hill.

>*Go back to Route 54A; continue heading north to the village of Penn Yan.*

PENN YAN HISTORIC DISTRICT 🔭

The name of the village was contrived from the first syllables of "Pennsylvania" and "Yankee," as most of the early settlers were Pennsylvanians and New Englanders (or Yankees). Stroll over to the historic district to see the broad range of architecturally significant examples of residential, commercial, industrial, civic and ecclesiastical structures. Highlights include the Birkett Mills, the Chronicle Building, Knapp Hotel, and the Castner House.

KEUKA RESTAURANT 🍴

12 Main Street, Penn Yan, NY 14527
Phone: (315) 536-5852
Online: www.keuka-restaurant.com

Hours: Daily, 11 AM to 10 PM
Corkage Fee: $8

You don't come to Penn Yan expecting molecular gastronomy. The food is conservative, small-town, American family restaurant fare – sandwiches, burgers, steaks, ribs, fish fry — nothing fancy, but it's done properly. The range of local beers on tap is worthy of hoopla.

SENECA FARMS ICE CREAM

2485 Route 54A, Penn Yan, NY 14527
Phone: (315) 536-4066
Online: www.senecafarmsny.com

When in Penn Yan, do as the locals do. After dinner, drive over to this 1950s-era ice cream parlor for a Turtle Sundae with homemade vanilla ice cream, hot fudge and hot caramel sauces, and toasted pecans. (Open March thru end of October)

BEST WESTERN VINEYARD INN & SUITES

142 Lake Street, Penn Yan, NY 14527
Phone: (315) 536-8473
Online: www.vineyardinnandsuites.com

Clean, comfortable, up-to-date accommodations within walking distance to downtown with fitness center, indoor heated pool, hot tub and business center. Rooms have a mini-fridge for the beer you purchased earlier in the day.

Sunday

PENN YAN DINER

131 East Elm Street, Penn Yan, NY 14527
Phone: (315) 536-6004
Online: www.pennyandiner.com

Breakfast here isn't anything you can't get most elsewhere, except for the sense of small town charm and the fact that you get to eat in a real diner.

It's a genuine slice of Americana, built in 1925 by the Richardson Dining Car factory, the first diner manufacturer in western New York, and it's had a succession of owners over the years, operated since 2012 by Carrie and Sean Ahearn. Freshly-brewed Finger Lakes Coffee Roasters' beans make a damn good cup of coffee.

>Take Route 54 to Route 14; make a right turn onto Route 14 heading south. Turn left onto Hansen Point Road.

CLIMBING BINES

511 Hansen Point Road (off Route 14), Penn Yan, NY 14527
Phone: (607) 745-0221
Online: www.climbingbineshopfarm.com

The stars have aligned on Climbing Bines, a hop farm and microbrewery, named for the vining plant that climbs by its shoots and wraps clockwise around its trellis, anchored on a farmstead settled by Chris Hansen's great-grandfather in 1905. Although most breweries don't have the real estate for growing their own ingredients, Chris, along with brewer Brian Karweck have developed a model farm-to-glass enterprise, utilizing 1500 estate-grown hop plants, a mix of 7 varieties, to lend flavors and aromas to a range of brews that are as distinctive and varied as those that grapes and soils give to wine. The "Pandemonium" beers (referencing an old name for Penn Yan in its less civilized past) use other local ingredients — barley, wheat, and rye — grown on nearby Peter Martin farm. The brewery's flagship Imperial IPA, made with earthy Cascade, Chinook and Nugget hops, stays true to the IPA's historical roots. Beers offered by the pint, in a flight, or in take-home growlers.

>Go back to Route 14 heading south; turn left onto Randall Crossing Road.

MILES CRAFT ALES AT MILES WINE CELLARS

168 Randall Crossing Road (off Route 14), Himrod, NY 14842
Phone: (607) 243-7742
Online: www.mileswinecellars.com

It's neither a winery nor a brewery, but this 200-year-old Greek Revival home, steeped in history, is one of the most scenic places to taste both local wine and beer. As an experienced and respected grower, Doug Miles devotes full time to the grapevines and relinquishes winemaking to Peter Bell at nearby Fox Run. Besides a sip or two of the wines, sample the small-batch ales at the Abandon Brewing facility in Penn Yan, then stroll the surrounding waterfront grounds.

>Get back onto Route 14 heading south.

STARKEY'S LOOKOUT

5428 New York 14, Dundee, NY 14837
Phone: (607) 678-4043
Online: www.starkeyslookout.com

Don't look for a hop farm or vineyard here, or for that matter, any brewing or winemaking facilities. A doctor and a lawyer partnered to build this mammoth tasting room — the size of a major hotel lobby — for contracted beers and wines. The beers are produced in the public market district of Rochester by the Rohrbach Brewing Company. Worth the stop to pick up a couple of 750-ml bottles of full-bodied Scotch Ale (the name given to a strong 19th century-style Edinburgh pale ale) with malty sweetness and 8.4% alcohol.

>Continue on Route 14 heading south to Watkins Glen.

ROOSTER FISH BREWPUB

223-301 North Franklin Street (Route 14), Watkins Glen, NY 14891
Phone: (607) 535-9797
Online: www.roosterfishbrewing.com

The drinking wing of the Wildflower Café is a chummy brewpub offering "Nut Brown Ale" and "Dog Tooth Pale Ale" among a dozen brews made with organic ingredients and Seneca Lake water. Lunch fare includes Buffalo wings, barbeque ribs, burgers and sausages, local organic steak, and pizza toppings on hand-stretched brewer's malt dough.

WATKINS GLEN STATE PARK

Walk off the calories with a hike into the most famous of the Finger Lakes

State Parks, with a reputation for leaving visitors spellbound. Within two miles, the glen's stream descends 400 feet past 200-foot cliffs, generating 19 waterfalls along its course. In 1933 President Franklin Roosevelt created the Civilian Conservation Corps in an effort to put unemployed men to work. They were responsible for building many of the present day pathways winding over and under waterfalls and through the spray of Cavern Cascade. The tunnels in the gorge were hand-cut in the rock. Wear comfortable shoes.

>From Route 14, just past the park entrance, turn left onto Route 329 (Old Corning Road), then right onto Walnut Road.

SENECA LODGE

3600 Walnut Road, Watkins Glen, NY 14891
Phone: (607) 535-2014
Online: www.senecalodge.com
Hours: Bar opens at 4 PM

Swing open the wide, creaking door and walk through a wood-paneled dining room. Pull up a stool at one of the most unusual bars you will ever see. Since 1948, the Seneca Lodge Tavern Room has been a gathering place for the drivers and crews of the Grand Prix races. Behind the bar, laurel wreaths from the Formula 1 races of the 1970s hang from hundreds of arrows shot into the wall by archers who frequent the lodge for archery championships. Suspended from the ceiling are tires from NASCAR champions. House-brewed beers on tap include Blonde Ale, Belgian-style, and an agressively-hopped IPA. This is a place to drink beer, not just taste it.

>Drive back to Route 14 heading south. At Horseheads, take Route 17 to Corning (about 40 minutes).

MARKET STREET BREWING COMPANY 🍴 🍺

63 West Market Street, Corning, NY 14830
Phone: (607) 936-2337
Online: www.936-beer.com

Settle in for dinner at Pelham and Theresa McClellan's beer-centered eatery, established in 1997. Located on Corning's quaint, bustling Market Street, the ambitious brewpub lures you in with an excellent core of five house-brewed beers, from the lighter Mad Bug Lager to the more robust English-style D'Artagnan Dark Ale, along with dishes like beer-braised bratwurst served with a side of honey-beer mustard. Weather permitting, alfresco dining available in the "biergarten."

RADISSON HOTEL CORNING

125 Denison Parkway East, Corning, NY 14830
Phone: (607) 962-5000
Online: www.radisson.com

Located in Corning's Gaffer District and convenient to the Corning Museum of Glass, the smoke-free and pet-friendly Radisson has an indoor pool and fitness center; all rooms include free Wi-Fi Internet access, large work desk, ergonomic chairs, flat-screen TV and room service from the hotel restaurant. Local beer and wine selections available at the Steuben Bar, located off the lobby.

Entry Point:

ITHACA

(SOUTH - EAST)

BEER TRAILS

DAY TRIP

ITHACA BAKERY 🍴 🛒

400 North Meadow Street (Route 13 North), Ithaca, NY 14850
Phone: (607) 273-7110
Online: www.ithacabakery.com

Hobnob with the locals at Ithaca Bakery. Turning out 1,000 bagels a day, along with artisan breads and pastries, the bakery is also a cafe, deli, and locally-popular gathering place. The self-service breakfast buffet bar is exceptional. Don't miss the glass display case loaded with beer-friendly cheeses for your road trip cooler, and take along the makings of a picnic at Stewart Park.

>Follow Route 13 heading north and take exit to Route 34 (East Shore Drive). Make a left turn onto Route 34, then an immediate left to the park entrance.

STEWART PARK 🔭

Gardner Parkway, Ithaca, NY 14850

On your way out of town, take a side trip (just off Route 34) to the park that hugs the southernmost point of Cayuga Lake, once the site of Wharton Brothers Studio and their production of "cliffhangers" during the silent film era. Today the municipal park provides tennis courts, playground, carousel, duck pond, spray pool, and bird sanctuary.

>As you exit the park, turn right onto Gibbs Drives and merge onto Route 13 South; turn left onto State Street.

FINGER LAKES BEVERAGE CENTER 🛒

605 West State Street, Ithaca, NY 14850
Phone: (607) 277-2337
Online: www.fingerlakesbeverage.com

The local, regional, and domestic selection is prodigious in this newly-expanded beverage emporium. You'll also find an astounding display of ales, pilsners, lagers, porters, stouts, and beers from every corner of the planet, in bottles, cans, and on draught at the 12-line growler station. Pat Moe's staff knows their brews, and are helpful with picking one to your liking. Every beer in the store is available for purchase as a single bottle; mix and match your own 6-packs.

>*Head back to Route 13 South and drive just past the city line; make a right turn onto Brewery Lane.*

ITHACA BEER COMPANY

606 Elmira Road (Route 13 South), Ithaca, NY 14850
Phone: (607) 273-0766
Online: www.ithacabeer.com

Just off Route 13 and behind a small industrial complex, Ithaca Beer Company, the "Granddaddy" of Finger Lakes craft breweries, cranks out provocative mainstays like Pale Ale and distinctively crafted brews like Nut Brown Ale and Flower Power IPA. In the process, they have built a loyal fan base that extends throughout the Finger Lakes and well beyond. The high-spirited Tap Room (and fair-weather outdoor beer garden) is open from 12 Noon (Wednesday thru Sunday) for soups, salads, burgers, and pizzas, served simply and expertly, molded by hand, and cooked in a wood-fired oven. Brewery tours are offered on Saturday and Sunday at the top of every hour, beginning at 12 Noon. Call ahead for tour reservation.

>*Get back onto Route 13, this time heading north out of Ithaca. It's a 30-minute drive to Cortland. Once in downtown, continue on Route 13 with a left turn onto Church Street, then another left onto Court Street.*

CORTLAND BEER COMPANY 🍺

16 Court Street, Cortland, NY 13045
Phone: (607) 662-4389
Online: www.cortlandbeer.com

This city of 20,000 is home to SUNY Cortland, a state university campus and summer training camp of the New York Jets. At the downtown Cortland Beer Company, Brewmaster Tom Scheffler, a Cornell Aggie, makes use of a 20-barrel brewing system, supplying kegs to many of the local bars and restaurants, and showcasing a wide variety of beers its own storefront taproom. "Industrial IPA" and "Firehouse Pale Ale" (its name inspired by the 1914 firehouse across the street from the brewery) follow the strong ale tradition, but the brewery's strength is most obvious in a rotating style of stouts (don't miss the stout crafted with locally roasted coffee beans). The most popular beers are available in 22-ounce bottles.

>*From Court Street, turn left onto Main Street, then an immediate right onto Route 13, heading south to the village of Dryden. Just past the entrance to Tompkins-Cortland Community College, turn right onto Ellis Drive.*

BACCHUS BREWING COMPANY 🍺

15 Ellis Drive, Dryden, NY 13053
Phone: (607) 844-8474
Online: www.bacchusbrewing.com

Anyone not on a hunt for serious craft beer might drive right past David McCune's unassuming microbrewery. Named for the Roman god of intoxication, the tasting room adjoins his physical therapy practice. Brewmaster Ritchie Shallcross, who earned his stripes at Ithaca Beer Company, oversees a copper-plated 7-barrel brewhouse, visible through a window in the tasting room. Among the solid offerings, compare his styles of "Bacchus IPA" and "Cyclhops," a single-malt, single-hop IPA. Growlers and mason jars to-go.

>*Get back onto Route 13 heading south. About 3 miles past the village, watch for the tall hop trellises at the entrance to Hopshire on the left.*

HOPSHIRE FARM & BREWERY 🍺

1771 Dryden Road (Route 13), Freeville, NY 13068
Phone: (607) 279-1243
Online: www.hopshire.com
Hours: Wednesday thru Friday at 4 PM; Saturday & Sunday from 12 Noon

The enterprise stays true to the slogan "beer from a farm, not a factory" with three acres of estate-grown hops of various varieties to supply this small-batch brewery. In a well-appointed, pleasantly-snug taproom that more resembles a winery tasting room, Randy Lacey, a mechanical engineer at Cornell, makes artfully-minded craft beers, sourcing interesting local ingredients, much like a painter selecting specific colors. "NearVarna" IPA is a hophead's delight, and "Beehave" is a refreshing blonde ale made with basswood honey. These and other inventive brews are offered in tastings and by the 8 or 10-ounce pour. Take home 64- or 32-ounce growlers, 16-ounce mason jars, or 750-ml bottles.

>Follow Route 13 heading south to Ithaca. Turn left onto West Buffalo Street, then right onto North Cayuga Street.

BANDWAGON BREW PUB 🍺 🍴

14 North Cayuga Street, Ithaca, NY 14850
Phone: (607) 319-0699
Online: www.bandwagonbeer.com
Dinner Hours: Monday thru Thursday from 5 PM; Weekends from 4 PM

Ithaca has more restaurants per capita than New York City, so choosing a place to eat is no easy task. But if your focus is on beer, take a few steps down into this basement-level, brick-walled brewpub offering ten rotating, beers on tap including five of its own and five from other microbreweries. These beers can be bold, experimental, sometimes unconventional, but always memorable. Order by the pint, or try a flight for variety's sake. The menu offers a local cheese plate, soups, salads, sandwiches, chicken wings, and an excellent ale-battered fish & chips.

>Take Cayuga Street heading north. Turn right onto Buffalo Street, then right onto Tioga Street. Drive to the corner of Seneca Street.

KILPATRICK'S PUBLICK HOUSE 🍺

130 East Seneca Street, Ithaca, NY 14850
Phone: (607) 273-2632
Online: www.kilpatrickspub.com

Distinctly Irish in both personality and conviviality, this hotel bar provides an opportunity to disconnect from the rest of the day's hectic pace. It's a melting pot of interesting characters and conversations, gathering at the granite-top bar for a range of beers -- from local favorites to the requisite Guinness Stout (beer flights available). If the bar is crowded, score one of the large private booths (each with its own TV).

HILTON GARDEN INN 🛏

130 East Seneca Street, Ithaca, NY 14850
Phone: (607) 277-8900
Online: www.hiltongardeninn.com

After that last beer of the day, you won't need to go very far to enjoy a comfortable night's sleep. Take the elevator to your room and sink into the "Sleep System" bed. All rooms are equipped with work desk, high-speed internet access, microwave and refrigerator. No need to use the in-room coffeemaker in the morning, there's a Starbucks at street level.

Entry Point:

ITHACA

(SOUTH - EAST)

BEER TRAILS

WEEKEND TOUR

BANDWAGON BREW PUB 🍺 🍴

14 North Cayuga Street, Ithaca, NY 14850
Phone: (607) 319-0699
Online: www.bandwagonbeer.com
Dinner Hours: Serving from 4 PM

Ithaca has more restaurants per capita than New York City, so choosing a place to eat is no easy task. But if your focus is on beer, take a few steps down into this basement-level, brick-walled brewpub offering ten rotating, beers on tap including five of its own and five from other microbreweries. These beers can be bold, experimental, sometimes unconventional, but always memorable. Order by the pint, or try a flight for variety's sake. The menu offers a local cheese plate, soups, salads, sandwiches, chicken wings, and an excellent ale-battered fish & chips.

>Take Cayuga Street heading north. Turn right onto Buffalo Street, then right onto Tioga Street. Drive to the corner of Seneca Street.

KILPATRICK'S PUBLICK HOUSE 🍺

130 East Seneca Street, Ithaca, NY 14850
Phone: (607) 273-2632
Online: www.kilpatrickspub.com

Distinctly Irish in both personality and conviviality, this hotel bar provides an opportunity to disconnect from the rest of the day's hectic pace. It's a melting pot of interesting characters and conversations, gathering at the granite-top bar for a range of beers -- from local favorites to the requisite Guinness Stout (beer flights available). If the bar is crowded, score one of the large private booths (each with its own TV).

HILTON GARDEN INN

130 E. Seneca Street, Ithaca, NY 14850
Phone: (607) 277-8900
Online: www.hiltongardeninn.com

After that last beer of the day, you won't need to go very far to enjoy a comfortable night's sleep. Take the elevator to your room and sink into the "Sleep System" bed. All rooms are equipped with work desk, high-speed internet access, microwave and refrigerator. No need to use the in-room coffeemaker in the morning, there's a Starbucks at street level.

Saturday

ITHACA BAKERY

400 North Meadow Street (Route 13 North), Ithaca, NY 14850
Phone: (607) 273-7110
Online: www.ithacabakery.com

Hobnob with the locals at Ithaca Bakery. Turning out 1,000 bagels a day, along with artisan breads and pastries, the bakery is also a cafe, deli, and locally-popular gathering place. The self-service breakfast buffet bar is exceptional. Don't miss the glass display case loaded with beer-friendly cheeses for your road trip cooler, and be sure to pick up a baguette and a few bottles of water to support your day of tastings.

>*From the bakery parking lot, turn right, then left onto Route 13 South; turn left onto State Street.*

FINGER LAKES BEVERAGE CENTER

605 West State Street, Ithaca, NY 14850
Phone: (607) 277-2337
Online: www.fingerlakesbeverage.com

The local, regional, and domestic selection is prodigious in this newly-expanded beverage emporium. You'll also find an astounding display of ales, pilsners, lagers, porters, stouts, and beers from every corner of the planet, in bottles, cans, and on draught at the 12-line growler station. Pat

Moe's staff knows their brews, and are helpful with picking one to your liking. Every beer in the store is available for purchase as a single bottle; mix and match your own 6-packs.

>*Follow West State Street (Route 79) heading west to Burdett (about 20 minutes) Just past the flashing red light, make a right turn onto Route 5, then another right onto Route 414.*

FINGER LAKES DISTILLING

4676 Route 414, Burdett, NY 14818
Phone: (607) 546-5510
Online: www.fingerlakesdistilling.com

The striking micro-distillery stands high above Seneca Lake, housing a custom-built 300-gallon, German-made Holstein pot still for the small-batch distillation of local grapes, including Gewürztraminer, Muscat and Catawba. Among the impressive elixirs is Seneca Drums, a London dry-style gin, energized with eleven botanicals, and McKenzie Rye Whiskey, distilled New York State grain, aged in charred casks and finished in wine barrels from local wineries.

>*Continue on Route 414 heading north along the eastern shore of Seneca Lake.*

WAGNER VALLEY BREWERY

9322 Route 414, Lodi, NY 14860
Phone: (607) 582-6450
Online: www.wagnerbrewing.com

The winery produces a total of thirty wines, all from the estate's 240 acres of vineyards, and all over the varietal map, but wine is not the only intriguing product offered here. The brew system at Wagner's is an imported 20-barrel, steam fired, four-vessel, German-style brewhouse, following the German Purity Law (or Reinheitsgebot), using only malt, hops, yeast, and water to make beer. Offering four standards and a half-dozen seasonal brews. Mainstays include "Sled Dog Doppelbock," an expressive, russet-hued tan-headed, Bavarian-style double bock, light and amber lagers, and an IPA, all available in 12-ounce bottles.

>Reverse course, heading south on Route 414.

DAÑO'S ON SENECA 🍴

9564 Route 414, Lodi, NY 14860
Phone: (607) 582-7555
Online: www.danosonseneca.com
Hours: Wednesday thru Monday, 12 Noon to 9 PM
Corkage Fee: $15

You brush past the chef's herb garden and peer into his kitchen as you enter the restaurant. Daño Hutnik is a superb chef who has played a major role in making the Finger Lakes a food as well as a wine region. The stage of his Austrian wine garden-inspired eatery features sleek counters stacked with pastries and filled with platters of rustic salads and main dishes. Daño's on Seneca is a Finger Lakes translation of the convivial roadside taverns (heurigers) in the wine-growing regions around Vienna. Servers help you assemble a meal to suit your appetite which you can enjoy inside the charming space or on an open-air patio with a view of the lake. Sip one of the brews from neighboring Wagner Valley Brewery and forget the cares of the world.

>Continue on Route 414 heading south.

TWO GOATS BREWING 🍺

5027 Route 414, Hector, NY 14818
Phone: (607) 546-2337
Online: www.twogoatsbrewing.com

This converted barn, just off the Seneca Lake wine trail, has a dive bar vibe without being a dive. No formal tastings here, just do as the locals do — belly up to the bar for an interesting range of house-brewed beers (as well as other beers on tap and even more in bottles), munch fresh-popped popcorn, and shoot darts. The best place to sip is on the wrap-around porch with a spectacular view of the lake and surrounding vineyards.

>Continue on Route 414 heading south to the village of Watkins Glen. At North Franklin Street, turn left; just past the park entrance, make a right turn onto Route 329 (Old Corning Road), then another right onto Walnut Road.

SENECA LODGE

3600 Walnut Road, Watkins Glen, NY 14891
Phone: (607) 535-2014
Online: www.senecalodge.com
Hours: Bar opens at 4 PM

Swing open the wide, creaking door and walk through a wood-paneled dining room. Pull up a stool at one of the most unusual bars you will ever see. Since 1948, the Seneca Lodge Tavern Room has been a gathering place for the drivers and crews of the Grand Prix races. Behind the bar, laurel wreaths from the Formula 1 races of the 1970s hang from hundreds of arrows shot into the wall by archers who frequent the lodge for archery championships. Suspended from the ceiling are tires from NASCAR champions. House-brewed beers on tap include Blonde Ale, Belgian-style, and an agressively-hopped IPA. This is a place to drink beer, not just taste it.

>*Drive back to North Franklin Street (Route 14); make a left turn heading north.*

CROOKED ROOSTER BREWPUB

223-301 North Franklin Street, Watkins Glen, NY 14891
Phone: (607) 535-9797
Online: www.roosterfishbrewing.com

The drinking wing of the Wildflower Café is a chummy brewpub offering "Nut Brown Ale" and "Dog Tooth Pale Ale" among a dozen brews made with organic ingredients and Seneca Lake water. Ambitious pub fare includes Buffalo wings, barbeque ribs, burgers and sausages, local organic steak, and pizza toppings on hand-stretched brewer's malt dough.

WATKINS GLEN HARBOR HOTEL

16 North Franklin Street, Watkins Glen, NY 14891
Phone: (607) 535-6116
Online: www.watkinsglenharborhotel.com

Nesting on the Southern-most point of Seneca Lake, hotel guestrooms are appointed with comfy pillow-topped mattresses covered with 310-thread count linens, plush duvet covers and feather pillows. Request a room with a view of the lake and enjoy a nightcap on your balcony.

Sunday

BLUE POINTE GRILLE

16 North Franklin Street (Route 14), Watkins Glen, NY 14891
Phone: (607) 535-6116
Online: www.watkinsglenharborhotel.com
Breakfast Hours: 7 AM to 11 AM

Start off your day with above average hotel dining room breakfast fare, including omelets, made-to-order eggs, steak & eggs, cereals, waffles, French toast, pancakes, and coffee or espresso. Ask for a table on the lakeside patio and enjoy the view overlooking Seneca harbor.

WATKINS GLEN STATE PARK

You loved the pancakes. Now walk them off at the most famous of the Finger Lakes State Parks, with a reputation for leaving visitors spellbound. Within two miles, the glen's stream descends 400 feet past 200-foot cliffs, generating 19 waterfalls along its course. In 1933 President Franklin Roosevelt created the Civilian Conservation Corps in an effort to put unemployed men to work. They were responsible for building many of the present day pathways winding over and under waterfalls and through the spray of Cavern Cascade. The tunnels in the gorge were hand cut in the rock. Wear comfortable shoes.

>Follow Route 14 heading south to Elmira (about 25 minutes), then follow Watkins Road into the village of Horseheads. Watkins Road becomes Main Street in Horseheads, then Lake Road in Elmira.

UPSTATE BREWING COMPANY

3028 Lake Road, Elmira, NY 14903
Phone: (607) 742-2750
Online: www.upstatebrewing.com

In a town known for its brewing history, co-brewers Ken Mortensen and

Mark Neumann operate an austere 7-barrel brewhouse, cranking out unfiltered IPW (India Pale Wheat), a cross between a traditional IPA and an American wheat beer, and "Common Sense," a pre-Prohibition-inspired, Kentucky-style brown ale — both available in 16-ounce cans by the 4-pack. (Cans are frowned upon by most craft breweries but in recent years have taken on an air of hipness, not to mention utility). Other rotating seasonal brews are sold in growlers. Cash or check only.

>*Follow Lake Road towards downtown Elmira. Make a right turn onto Clemens Center Parkway Extension, left onto Grand Central Avenue, then right onto Clemens Center Parkway. Turn right onto East Church Street, then right onto Davis Street.*

HORIGAN'S TAVERN 🍴

365 Davis Street, Elmira, NY 14901
Phone: (607) 732-6625

For a glass of beer and a few helpings of eccentricity, meander into downtown Elmira for lunch at Horigan's Tavern. A fixture in the city's historic Near Westside Neighborhood, Horigan's began life as a drugstore, then became a saloon with the repeal of Prohibition. It's changed hands a few times since then, but what remains constant is its legacy as a great local hangout with the best burgers in town and a dependable selection of local microbrews on tap.

>*Drive back to Church Street, turn left and drive across town to Route 86 heading west. Take Horseheads Exit 53, turn left onto Grand Central Avenue, then right onto Chemung Street to the corner of Kendall Street.*

BIRDLAND BREWING COMPANY 🍺

1015 Kendall Street, Horseheads, NY 14845
Phone: (607) 769-2337
Online: www.birdlandbrewingco.com

From homebrew hobby to the beer business, mechanical technician Dennis Edwards transformed a carwash into a brewery, christened after the section of town where all the streets are named for birds (Dennis lives on Oriole Street). Though the space is small and minimalistic, customers hang around. They chat with each other, taste the selections on tap and talk about beer. Among the flagship offerings, "Kewlerskald," is a well-balanced, full flavored amber ale and "Red Wing," is a rich red ale that satisfies like a big red wine and ends with a crisp finish like a white. 32- and 64-ounce growlers-to-go.

>*Drive back to Chemung Street, make a left turn onto Grand Central Avenue, then right onto West Franklin Street. Pass through Hanover Square, bearing left onto Old Ithaca Road.*

HORSEHEADS BREWING 🍺

250 Old Ithaca Road, Horseheads, NY 14845
Phone: (607) 739-8468
Online: www.horseheadsbrewing.com

After marching 450-miles in a massive campaign to destroy villages of the native Iroquois tribes who had taken up arms against the American revolutionaries, forces of General John Sullivan were obliged to dispose of a large number of sick and disabled horses. The natives collected the skulls and arranged them along a trail which became known as the "valley of the horses' heads." Just outside the town of Horseheads, this place is as down-home as you can get. Opened in 2007, the taproom is truly low-key — there's just a simple counter on one end and a glass-door refrigerator full beer on the other. But Ed Samchisen's big, full-bodied brews are consistent award winners in craft beer competitions. Standard pours include an IPA, Chemung Canal Towpath Ale (a cream ale), and Horseheads Hefe, a unique take on the traditional Bavarian classic, available in large-format bottles or by the fresh-drawn growler.

>*Continue on Old Ithaca Road to the roundabout; pick up Route 13 heading north to Ithaca (about 25 minutes)*

1853 COVERED BRIDGE 🔭

Take a short detour off Route 13, just a few miles before Ithaca and drive through the oldest surviving covered bridge still open to daily vehicular traffic (built by Samuel Hamm and Sons and dedicated to Elijah Moore, the son of an early settler). It crosses the west branch of the Cayuga Creek in a single span of 115 feet.

>Get back onto Route 13 heading north to Ithaca. Turn left onto Brewery Lane.

ITHACA BEER COMPANY 🍺 🍴

606 Elmira Road (Route 13 South), Ithaca, NY 14850
Phone: (607) 273-0766
Online: www.ithacabeer.com

It's just off Route 13 and behind a small industrial complex. Chances are this local gathering place will be packed with everyone from kids to beer geeks when you get here. This "Granddaddy" of Finger Lakes craft breweries has built a loyal fan base that extends throughout the Finger Lakes and beyond, cranking out provocative mainstays like Pale Ale and distinctively crafted brews like Nut Brown Ale and Flower Power IPA. The Tap Room hums and at times roars with the sound of people having a good time. All the beers are superb; drink in flights so you get to sample as many as possible. Offerings from the kitchen include soups, salads, wood-fired pizzas, and burgers.

>Follow Route 13 heading north into the city; turn right onto Green Street; keep left, then turn left onto East State Street (East Martin Luther King Jr. Street), then right onto North Aurora Street.

ITHACA ALE HOUSE 🍺

111 North Aurora Street, Ithaca, NY 14850
Phone: (607) 256-7977
Online: www.ithacaalehouse.com

Before settling in for the night, head over to this Aurora Street beer bar and choose from 20 brews on tap, mostly local and regional. A seat at one of the sidewalk tables out front is prime people-watching territory.

>Take Aurora Street heading south (Route 96B) up South Hill.

LA TOURELLE

1150 Danby Road (Route 96B), Ithaca, NY 14850
Phone: (800) 765-1492

Online: www.latourelle.com

This lovely retreat is nestled on seventy rolling acres just past Ithaca College, atop South Hill. Expertly managed by Scott Wiggins, La Tourelle pampers guests with feather beds in well-appointed rooms. The property includes 4 tennis courts, hiking trails, and spa with a range of services including "vino-therapy" (powdered regional grape seeds rubbed into the skin).

Pitched on the grounds of La Tourelle, Firelight Camps provides an overnight experience for the more adventurous. It's called "glamping" (glamorous camping). Sleep outdoors in a safari tent and awaken to a continental breakfast with locally-roasted "campfire coffee." More info at www.firelightcamps.com.

Entry Point:

SKANEATELES

(NORTH - EAST)

BEER TRAILS

DAY TRIP

BLUEWATER GRILL

11 West Genesee Street (Route 20), Skaneateles, NY 13152
Phone: (315) 685-6600
Hours: Open for breakfast at 8 AM

Perched on the north shore of Skaneateles Lake, Bluewater offers a full breakfast menu with all the necessities. Ask for a table on the outside deck overlooking the bluish-green waters of the lake and imbibe some local color.

SKANEATELES

It's a charming and somewhat eccentric village nestled at the north end of the lake, where antique shops and boutiques flourish in the business district (malls and fast-food outlets are outlawed). Clift Park in the heart of the village has a long pier that walks out onto the lake, used for fishing by many locals and picture-taking by visitors.

>Follow Route 20 heading west to Auburn.

AUBURN

The "Genesee Beer" sign, 26 feet high and 48 feet wide (85 feet from the ground to the top), was erected atop the six-story building then called Auburn Music Center (now Speno Music) at 3 East Genesee Street in 1952. The sign is a landmark for motorists heading to or through downtown Auburn, maintained by the Rochester-based brewery to highlight its historic place in Upstate New York's beer culture. (Pick up a six-pack of "Genny" Cream Ale at the D&L Truck Stop on Owasco Street before leaving town).

>Turn left onto South Street (Route 34), then another left onto Lincoln Street to Loop Road.

THE GOOD SHEPHERDS BREWING COMPANY

31 Loop Road, Auburn, NY 13021
Phone: (315) 406-6498
Online: www.facebook.com/ShepherdsBrewing

A promising newcomer, Garrett Shepherd honed his craft through the trials and tribulations of home brewing, apprenticed at CB Craft Brewers in Honeoye Falls, built an arsenal of UK-inspired recipes for this fledgling, single-barrel nanobrewery, and created a "rathskeller" next to the town's tattoo parlor. His small scale affords Garrett an unusual degree of freedom to experiment with a range of personally-crafted beers, including Auburn Amber, brewed with hops grown in nearby Skaneateles.

>*Follow Loop Road to South Street. Turn right onto South Street, then left onto Route 20. Heading west out of Auburn, Route 20 becomes Routes 5&20; continue to Seneca Falls (about 20 minutes).*

MONTEZUMA WINERY ⓦ

2981 Routes 5&20, Seneca Falls, NY 13148
Phone: (315) 568-8190
Online: www.montezumawinery.com

The Martin family translates the fragrant essence of apples, strawberries, blueberries, raspberries, cranberries, peaches, plums, and rhubarb from local farms and orchards into stand-alone fruit wines that provide a taste of fruit at the peak of the season. A sister operation, Hidden Marsh Distillery, produces liqueurs, vodka, and brandy made with honey, apples, and other seasonal fruits.

>*Continue on Routes 5&20 heading west into the hamlet of Seneca Falls.*

SENECA FALLS 👀

Residents claim that when director Frank Capra visited Seneca Falls in 1945, he was inspired to model fictional Bedford Falls in the holiday film classic *It's a Wonderful Life* after their town. And no visit to this town is complete without a walk across the steel truss bridge over the Cayuga-Seneca Canal, a close match to the bridge that George Bailey jumped from to save Clarence the angel.

>*Continue on Routes 5&20 heading west.*

ABIGAIL'S RESTAURANT 🍴

1978 Routes 5&20, Waterloo, NY 13165
Phone: (315) 539-9300
Online: www.abigailsrestaurant.com
Lunch Hours: Monday thru Friday, 11 AM to 2 PM

The address is Waterloo, but watch for Abigail's just outside of Seneca Falls. Documentary filmmaker Matt Reynolds and a team of judges spent 16 days traveling 2,627 miles and trying 270 culinary interpretations of chicken wings from 72 bars and restaurants along the "Wing Belt" of upstate New York, Pennsylvania, Vermont, and Ontario. By the end of their quest, the "Blue Bayou" wings created by chef Columbus Marshall Grady at Abigail's were named the world's best wings. Pair your order with a well-chilled bottle from CB Craft Brewers in Honeoye Falls.

>*Continue on Routes 5&20 heading west to Canandaigua (about 45 minutes).*

NAKED DOVE BREWING 🍺

4048 Routes 5&20, Canandaigua, NY 14424
Phone: (585) 396-2537
Online: www.nakeddovebrewing.com

After earning masterbrewer's credentials at Rohrbach, Custom Brewcafters, and High Falls Brewing, Dave Schlosser set out on his own, building a 15-barrel system and launching Naked Dove Brewing in 2010. While the atmosphere is basic and unassuming, the beers aspire to greater things. Standard offerings, an IPA, porter, amber ale and black raspberry ale, are supplemented with seasonal and specialty brews made with hops sourced from Peterson Farms in Seneca Castle, just eight miles from the brewery. "Expose yourself to Naked Dove" is the motto here, and tap room tasting flights are served in a take-home glass with the brewery logo.

>*Continue on Routes 5&20 heading west. Turn right onto South Main Street, right onto Niagara Street, then another right onto Pleasant Street.*

TWISTED RAIL BREWING COMPANY 🍺

20 Pleasant Street, Canandaigua, NY 14424
Phone: (585) 797-7437
Online: www.twistedrailbrewing.com

They always seem happy to have visitors. This is a "naked brewery" with brewing equipment on full display at the far end of the space, allowing patrons to watch the manufacturing of beers like Cabin Killer IPA among its core lineup, and also special one-offs such as a Wild Hop Ale made with hops picked along the Genesee Valley Greenway Trail near Caledonia. In keeping with its setting in a 100-year-old train depot (shared with the Beehive Brewpub), partners John McMullen, Mike McMullen and Nathan Sirvent have installed tap handles modeled after old railroad spikes and an actual rail that serves as a footrest. Step up to the cherry-wood-topped bar for flights and pints, with 64-ounce growlers-to-go.

>Return to Routes 5&20 via South Main Street, heading east to Geneva (about 20 minutes); turn left onto Castle Street.

LAKE DRUM BREWING 🍺

16 East Castle Street, Geneva, NY 14456
Phone: (315) 789-1200
Online: www.lakedrumbrewing.com

Some believe those distant booms or "drums" over the deep, still waters of Seneca Lake are messages from the Iroquois who once inhabited the area (although scientists explain they are simply the result of geothermal reactions). The legend inspires the name of a nanobrewery start-up, the first operation to produce alcoholic beverages in the city since Prohibition. Victor Pultinas and Jenna LaVita lend their winemaking expertise, fermenting "farmhouse style" brews in red wine barrels with brettanomyces for the sour notes and attractive complexity common in Belgian ales. Beers and house-made ciders offered by the tasting flights, by the pint, and in growlers-to-go.

>Get back onto Routes 5&20 heading east to Skaneateles (about 50 minutes).

SHERWOOD INN

26 West Genesee Street (Route 20), Skaneateles, NY 13152
Phone: (315) 685-3405
Online: www.thesherwoodinn.com
Corkage Fee: $20

Known as the "Stage Coach King," Isaac Sherwood founded stage lines from Albany to Buffalo which led to the rapid growth of industry and commerce in the Finger Lakes region, and the inn he built for weary stagecoach travelers in 1807 has provided local hospitality ever since. Set in the heart of the village overlooking the lake. Ask for a table in The Tavern for more informal dining (with wood-burning fireplace in the winter months) or on the Lakeview Porch, and dine on America classic such as Yankee Pot Roast and Herb-Roasted Chicken along with several local beers on tap, including "Skaneateles Light," brewed exclusively for the Sherwood by Empire Brewing in Syracuse, produced with water from Skaneateles Lake. After dinner, take a stroll to Clift Park across the street, then repair to one of the 15 comfortable, antique-appointed guest rooms, each carefully restored and decorated to retain the setting's period charm.

Entry Point:

SKANEATELES

(NORTH - EAST)

BEER TRAILS

WEEKEND TOUR

Friday

ROSALIE'S CUCINA

841 West Genesee Street (Route 20), Skaneateles, NY 13152
Phone: (315) 685-2200
Online: www.rosaliescucina.com
Hours: 5 PM to 10 PM
Corkage Fee: $20 (limit 2 bottles per table)

Next door to Mirbeau, this remarkable restaurant is the brainstorm of Auburn native Phil Romano, who earned a national reputation with multi-unit theme eateries including Romano's Macaroni Grill. Rosalie's has the same engaging Italian fare, only it's slightly more upscale and a bit pricier. It's difficult to say what's best about Rosalie's — the bustling, high-energy setting, the well-trained servers, or the terrific food. Beer selections from Middle Ages Brewing Company in nearby Syracuse.

FINGER LAKES LODGING

834 West Genesee Street (Route 20), Skaneateles, NY 13152
Phone: (315) 217-0222
Online: www.fingerlakeslodging.com

Not as luxurious as Mirbeau, its sister property across the street, this former motel has been upgraded with Adirondack flourishes and clean, comfortable rooms. Best bet for an overnight stay, plus you can enjoy the spa amenities at Mirabeau for a small fee without the price of staying there.

Saturday

BLUEWATER GRILL

11 West Genesse Street, Skaneateles, NY 13152
Phone: (315) 685-6600
Hours: Sunday - Thursday, 8 AM to 9 PM; Friday & Saturday, 8 AM to 10 PM

Perched on the north shore of Skaneateles Lake, Bluewater offers a full breakfast menu with all the necessities. Ask for a table on the outside deck overlooking the bluish-green waters of the lake and imbibe some local color.

SKANEATELES

It's a charming and somewhat eccentric village nestled at the north end of the lake, where antique shops and boutiques flourish in the business district (malls and fast-food outlets are outlawed). Clift Park in the heart of the village has a long pier that walks out onto the lake, used for fishing by many locals and picture-taking by visitors.

>Follow Route 20 heading west to Auburn.

AUBURN

The "Genesee Beer" sign, 26 feet high and 48 feet wide (85 feet from the ground to the top), was erected atop the six-story building then called Auburn Music Center (now Speno Music) at 3 East Genesee Street in 1952. The sign is a landmark for motorists heading to or through downtown Auburn, maintained by the Rochester-based brewery to highlight its historic place in Upstate New York's beer culture. (Pick up a six-pack of "Genny" Cream Ale at the D&L Truck Stop on Owasco Street before leaving town).

>Turn left onto South Street (Route 34), then another left onto Lincoln Street to Loop Road.

THE GOOD SHEPHERDS BREWING COMPANY

31 Loop Road, Auburn, NY 13021
Phone: (315) 406-6498
Online: www.facebook.com/ShepherdsBrewing

A promising newcomer, Garrett Shepherd honed his craft through the trials and tribulations of home brewing, apprenticed at CB Craft Brewers in Honeoye Falls, built an arsenal of UK-inspired recipes for this fledgling, single-barrel nanobrewery, and created a "rathskeller" in the old Nolan's Shoe Store. His small scale affords Garrett an unusual degree of freedom to experiment with a range of personally-crafted beers, wooing locals and beer tourists with tasting flights and growlers-to-go.

>*Follow Loop Road to South Street. Turn right onto South Street, then left onto Route 20. Heading west out of Auburn, Route 20 becomes Routes 5&20; continue to Seneca Falls (about 20 minutes).*

MONTEZUMA WINERY 🍷

2981 Routes 5&20, Seneca Falls, NY 13148
Phone: (315) 568-8190
Online: www.montezumawinery.com

The Martin family translates the fragrant essence of apples, strawberries, blueberries, raspberries, cranberries, peaches, plums, and rhubarb from local farms and orchards into stand-alone wines that provide a taste of fruit at the peak of the season. A sister operation, Hidden Marsh Distillery, produces liqueurs, vodka, and brandy made with honey, apples, and other seasonal bounty.

>*Continue on Routes 5&20 heading west into the hamlet of Seneca Falls.*

SENECA FALLS 🔭

Residents claim that when director Frank Capra visited Seneca Falls in 1945, he was inspired to model fictional Bedford Falls in the holiday film classic *It's a Wonderful Life* after their town. And no visit to this town is complete without a walk across the steel truss bridge over the Cayuga-Seneca Canal, a close match to the bridge that George Bailey jumped from to save Clarence the angel.

>*Continue on Routes 5&20 heading west to Waterloo.*

MAC'S DRIVE-IN 🍴

1166 Routes 5&20, Waterloo, NY 13165
Phone: (315) 539-3064
Online: www.macsdrivein.net
Hours: 10:30 AM to 10 PM (Closed Monday)

The heyday of drive-ins may be decades in the past, but drive-in culture still flourishes a half mile west of the village of Waterloo. Opened in 1961, when the juke box played "Let's Twist Again," the MacDougal family faithfully maintains car-hop service from a menu which includes hamburgers, French fries, and "chicken-in-a-basket" washed down with root beer and milkshakes. The ice cream window offers sundaes and banana splits. (Eat-in dining available).

>*Continue on Routes 5&20 heading west to Geneva. Turn left onto Route 96A; drive 4 miles, then turn right onto Lerch Road.*

WAR HORSE BREWING COMPANY AT THREE BROTHERS WINERY

623 Lerch Road, Geneva, NY 14456
Phone: (315) 585-4432
Online: www.3brotherswinery.com/war-horse

The Three Brothers venture is more like an amusement park than a winery or brewery. It's rustic, quaint, and all about entertainment. If fact, while they do grow grapes and make wines, the "War Horse Brewing Company" is not a brewery at all, but a sales room for beers produced by CB Craft Brewers in Honeoye Falls. If you can weave your way past the crowds at the wine slushie stand, sample offerings including the Riesling Ale — an Americanized version of a Hefeweizen spiked with Riesling grape juice. It's a refreshing tipple when served with a lemon wedge. Available by the growler or 22-ounce bottle.

>*Drive back to Route 96A; turn right, heading south. At Lodi, keep straight onto Route 414 heading south.*

WAGNER VALLEY BREWERY

9322 Route 414, Lodi, NY 14860
Phone: (607) 582-6450
Online: www.wagnerbrewing.com

The winery produces a total of thirty wines, all from the estate's 240 acres of vineyards, and all over the varietal map, but wine is not the only intriguing product offered here. The brew system at Wagner's is an imported 20-barrel, steam fired, four-vessel, German-style brewhouse, following the

German Purity Law (or Reinheitsgebot), using only malt, hops, yeast, and water to make beer. Offering four standards and a half-dozen seasonal brews. Mainstays include "Sled Dog Doppelbock," an expressive, russet-hued tan-headed, Bavarian-style double bock, light and amber lagers, and an IPA, all available in 12-ounce bottles.

>*Continue on Route 414 heading south along the eastern shore of Seneca Lake.*

TWO GOATS BREWING

5027 Route 414, Hector, NY 14818
Phone: (607) 546-2337
Online: www.twogoatsbrewing.com

This converted barn, just off the Seneca Lake wine trail, has a dive bar vibe without being a dive. No formal tastings here, just do as the locals do — belly up to the bar for an interesting range of house-brewed beers (as well as other beers on tap and even more in bottles), munch fresh-popped popcorn, and shoot darts. The best place to sip is on the wrap-around porch with a spectacular view of the lake and surrounding vineyards. Skip the roast beef sandwich (the only item on the menu), and save your appetite for the next stop.

>*Continue of Route 414 heading south; turn left onto Tug Hollow Road (County Route 5), then left onto Lake Street to the stop light. Drive straight ahead, following Route 79 to Ithaca. Turn left onto Route 13 South, drive just past the city limit; turn right onto Brewery Lane.*

ITHACA BEER COMPANY

606 Elmira Road (Route 13 South), Ithaca, NY 14850
Phone: (607) 273-0766
Online: www.ithacabeer.com

It's just off Route 13 and behind a small industrial complex. Chances are this local gathering place will be packed with everyone from kids to beer geeks when you get here. This "Granddaddy" of Finger Lakes craft breweries has built a loyal fan base that extends throughout the Finger Lakes and beyond, cranking out provocative mainstays like Pale Ale and distinctively crafted brews like Nut Brown Ale and Flower Power IPA. The

Tap Room hums and at times roars with the sound of people having a good time. All the beers are superb; drink in flights so you get to sample as many as possible. Offerings from the kitchen include soups, salads, wood-fired pizzas, and burgers.

>*Get back onto Route 13 heading north in to the city. Turn right onto Buffalo Street, then right onto Tioga Street. Drive to the corner of Seneca Street.*

KILPATRICK'S PUBLICK HOUSE 🍺

130 East Seneca Street, Ithaca, NY 14850
Phone: (607) 273-2632
Online: www.kilpatrickspub.com

Distinctly Irish in both personality and conviviality, this hotel bar provides an opportunity to disconnect from the rest of the day's hectic pace. It's a melting pot of interesting characters and conversations, gathering at the granite-top bar for a range of beers -- from local favorites to the requisite Guinness Stout (beer flights available). If the bar is crowded, score one of the large private booths (each with its own TV).

HILTON GARDEN INN 🛏

130 East Seneca Street, Ithaca, NY 14850
Phone: (607) 277-8900
Online: www.hiltongardeninn.com

After that last beer of the day, you won't need to go very far to enjoy a comfortable night's sleep. Take the elevator to your room and sink into the "Sleep System" bed. All rooms are equipped with work desk, high-speed internet access, microwave and refrigerator. No need to use the in-room coffeemaker in the morning, there's a Starbucks at street level.

Sunday

ITHACA BAKERY 🍴 🛒

400 North Meadow Street (Route 13 North), Ithaca, NY 14850
Phone: (607) 273-7110
Online: www.ithacabakery.com

Hobnob with the locals at Ithaca Bakery. Turning out 1,000 bagels a day, along with artisan breads and pastries, the bakery is also a cafe, deli, and the best place to kick off your day. Nibble from the self-service breakfast buffet bar and pick up the makings of a picnic at Stewart Park.

>Follow Route 13 heading north and take exit to Route 34. Make a left turn onto Route 34, then an immediate left to the park entrance.

STEWART PARK 🔭

It was once the site of Wharton Brothers Studio, where Theodore and Leopold Wharton produced over 100 silent films from 1914 through 1919, an era when moviemaking was an emerging art form and burgeoning industry. Today the lakeside municipal park offers several facilities including tennis courts, playground with play structures including carousel, athletic fields, duck pond, spray pool, municipal golf course, and bird sanctuary.

>Leaving the park, take a right turn to Route 13 South; turn left onto State Street.

FINGER LAKES BEVERAGE CENTER 🛒

605 West State Street, Ithaca, NY 14850
Phone: (607) 277-2337
Online: www.fingerlakesbeverage.com
Sunday Hours: Noon to 7 PM

The local, regional, and domestic selection is prodigious in this newly-expanded beverage emporium. You'll also find an astounding display of ales, pilsners, lagers, porters, stouts, and beers from every corner of the planet, in bottles, cans, and on draught at the 12-line growler station. Pat

Moe's staff knows their brews, and are helpful with picking one to your liking. Every beer in the store is available for purchase as a single bottle; mix and match your own 6-packs.

>*Get back onto Route 13 North. Ten minutes or so out of town, watch for the tall hop trellises at the entrance to Hopshire on the right.*

HOPSHIRE FARM & BREWERY 🍺

1771 Dryden Road (Route 13), Freeville, NY 13068
Phone: (607) 279-1243
Online: www.hopshire.com

The enterprise stays true to the slogan "beer from a farm, not a factory" with three acres of estate-grown hops of various varieties to supply this small-batch brewery. In a well-appointed taproom that more resembles a winery tasting room, Randy Lacey, a mechanical engineer at Cornell, makes artfully-minded craft beers, sourcing interesting local ingredients, much like a painter selecting specific colors. "NearVarna" IPA is a hop-head's delight, and "Beehave" is a refreshing blonde ale made with basswood honey. These and other inventive brews are offered in tastings and by the 8 or 10-ounce pour. Take home 64- or 32-ounce growlers, 16-ounce mason jars, or 750-ml bottles.

>*Continue north on Route 13 to the village of Dryden.*

TODI'S PIZZERIA 🍴

22 West Main Street, Dryden, NY 13053
Phone: (607) 844-4343
Online: www.todispizza.com

It's a family owned and run, small-town pizza joint, and locals will tell you that Todi's is the best place to go for an authentic, prepared-by-hand, tomato pie. Beer and pizza go together as naturally as, well, pizza and beer.

> *Follow Route 13 heading north. Just past the center of the village turn left onto Ellis Drive.*

BACCHUS BREWING COMPANY 🍺

15 Ellis Drive, Dryden, NY 13053
Phone: (607) 844-8474
Online: www.bacchusbrewing.com

Anyone not on a hunt for serious craft beer might drive right past David McCune's unassuming microbrewery. Named for the Roman god of intoxication, the tasting room adjoins his physical therapy practice. Brewmaster Ritchie Shallcross, who earned his stripes at Ithaca Beer Company, oversees a copper-plated 7-barrel brewhouse, visible through a window in the tasting room. Among the solid offerings, compare his styles of "Bacchus IPA" and "Cyclhops," a single-malt, single-hop IPA. Growlers and mason jars to-go.

>*Get back onto Route 13 heading north to Cortland. Once in downtown, continue on Route 13 with a left turn onto Church Street, then another left onto Court Street.*

CORTLAND BEER COMPANY 🍺

16 Court Street, Cortland, NY 13045
Phone: (607) 662-4389
Online: www.cortlandbeer.com

This city of 20,000 is home to SUNY Cortland, a state university campus and summer training camp of the New York Jets. At the downtown Cortland Beer Company, Brewmaster Tom Scheffler, a Cornell Aggie, makes use of a 20-barrel brewing system, supplying kegs to many of the local bars and restaurants, and showcasing a wide variety of beers its own storefront taproom. "Industrial IPA" and "Firehouse Pale Ale" (its name inspired by the 1914 firehouse across the street from the brewery) follow the strong ale tradition, but the brewery's strength is most obvious in a rotating style of stouts (don't miss the stout crafted with locally roasted coffee beans). The most popular beers are available in 22-ounce bottles.

>*From Court Street, turn right onto Main Street (which becomes Route 11), follow Route 11 for about 2 1/2 miles, then make a left turn onto to Route 41 heading north to Skaneateles (about 30 minutes). At Route 20, make a left turn into the village.*

SHERWOOD INN

26 West Genesee Street (Route 20), Skaneateles, NY 13152
Phone: (315) 685-3405
Online: www.thesherwoodinn.com

Known as the "Stage Coach King," Isaac Sherwood founded stage lines from Albany to Buffalo which led to the rapid growth of industry and commerce in the Finger Lakes region, and the inn he built for weary stagecoach travelers in 1807 has provided local hospitality ever since. Set in the heart of the village overlooking the lake. Ask for a table in The Tavern for more informal dining (with wood-burning fireplace in the winter months) or on the Lakeview Porch, and dine on America classic such as Yankee Pot Roast and Herb-Roasted Chicken along with several local beers on tap, including "Skaneateles Light," brewed exclusively for the Sherwood by Empire Brewing in Syracuse, produced with water from Skaneateles Lake. After dinner, take a stroll to Clift Park across the street, then repair to one of the 15 comfortable, antique-appointed guest rooms, each carefully restored and decorated to retain the setting's period charm.

Entry Point:

CANANDAIGUA

(NORTH - WEST)

SCENIC & HISTORIC

DAY TRIP

LAFAYETTE RESTAURANT

408 Lakeshore Drive, Canandaigua, NY 14424
Phone: (585) 394-5383
Online: www.lafayettemotelandrestaurant.com

Breakfast at this 50-year-old local institution is a special pleasure. In a homey, diner-style setting, plates are piled high with eggs, waffles, pancakes, French toast, homemade breads, cinnamon buns, and fat pies. The staff is friendly and service is usually pretty quick. Take home a bag of house-blend coffee beans.

>Drive west on Lakeshore Drive. Park along the lakefront near the Culinary Center.

KERSHAW PARK

A bedroom community for nearby Rochester and historically a popular summer retreat for wealthy city folk (Humphrey Bogart's family maintained a summertime cottage on the lake), Canandaigua was built on the site of a Seneca Indian village, becoming an important railroad junction and home port for several steamboats by the mid-19th century. Between 1920 and 1936, old cars among other things were dumped in the lake here to anchor the earth and rocks used to make Kershaw Park. Stroll along the lakefront walkways or have an impromptu picnic at the park, just off Lakeshore Drive, the original shoreline of the lake.

NEW YORK WINE & CULINARY CENTER

800 S. Main Street, Canandaigua, NY 14424
Phone: (585) 394-7070
Online: www.nywcc.com

Keep walking. You're headed to the New York Wine & Culinary Center, northwest gateway to the bounty of food and wine produced throughout the state. The Center includes a demonstration theater, hands-on kitchen, bistro, gift boutique, and tasting room where you can acquaint yourself with wines and beers from around the state.

>Drive north on Main Street (Route 21), turn right onto Howell Street, then left onto Charlotte Street.

SONNENBERG MANSION AND GARDENS

151 Charlotte Street, Canandaigua, NY 14424
Phone: (585) 394-4922
Online: www.sonnenberg.org

Spend some peaceful moments at Sonnenberg. Fred Thompson, a wealthy banker, founded the First National Bank of the City of New York (now called Citibank). In 1931, his Canandaigua estate was sold to the Federal Government for use as a hospital. In 1970, a non-profit called Friends of Sonnenberg acquired the property, and began restoration. Most of the gardens are rose gardens with shrubs and trellises and rocks and ponds. Seasonally, flowers like tulips and pansies and mums will come into focus. The mansion is extensive with rooms of historical momentos and period pieces of furniture and furnishings. Adult admission is $12 (seniors $10).

>Drive back to Main Street (Route 21). Make a right turn onto Main and drive 3 blocks.

GRANGER HOMESTEAD & CARRIAGE MUSEUM

295 N. Main Street, Canandaigua, NY 14424
Phone: (585) 394-1472
Online: www.grangerhomestead.org

The legacy of the four generations of the Granger family lives on through the preservation of their early 19th century Federal-style home. Tour the living quarters, then head over to the antique carriage museum, a collection of horse-drawn carriages, ranging from luxury to commercial.

>Take Main Street (Route 21) heading south to Routes 5&20 and turn left, heading east to Geneva.

RED JACKET ORCHARDS 🛒

957 Routes 5&20, Geneva, NY 14456
Phone: (315) 781-2749
Online: www.redjacketorchards.com

Finger Lakes apples have a zest from the colder climate and high-acid soil, elevating malic acid, which gives the fruit its high-profile flavor. Red

Jacket Orchards, in the hands of the Nicholson family since 1958, grows sixteen varieties of apples, including heirloom varieties that allow you to taste history. Try the Newton Pippins, a favorite of Benjamin Franklin. The farm store is stocked with a wide range of fruits, vegetables, jams, jellies, crackers and Amish goods.

>Continue on Routes 5&20 heading east to downtown. Turn left onto Castle Street, then left onto Exchange Street.

OPUS ESPRESSO AND WINE BAR ✏️

486 Exchange Street, Geneva, NY 14456
Phone: (315) 759-5388
Online: www.opusfingerlakes.com
Hours: Monday thru Friday, 7 AM to 4 PM; Saturday, 8 AM to 2 PM

This bouncy, obliging place has a joyfulness to it, offering well-crafted sustenance that speaks to the senses as well as the appetite. A selection of wines by the glass, half-glass, or bottle make this snug spot popular with nibblers and sippers. Service is expert and agile. If it's grab-and-go you have in mind, a server will fill your hamper with the makings of a first-rate picnic.

GENEVA HISTORICAL SOCIETY 🔭

543 South Main Street, Geneva, NY 14456
Phone: (315) 789-5151
Online: www.genevahistoricalsociety.com

Charles Butler, a Geneva attorney, built the Federal-style home in 1829. Phineas Prouty, a local merchant, purchased the home in 1842, and the property remained in the Prouty family for 60 years. Beverly Chew, the great-grandson of Phineas Prouty, then purchased the home in 1921, conveying the family residence to the Geneva Historical Society in 1960. The building houses the Geneva History Museum (exhibits are self-guided).

>From downtown Geneva, drive back to Routes 5&20 heading west, then take Route 14 heading south.

FOX RUN VINEYARDS

670 Route 14, Penn Yan, NY 14527
Phone: (800) 636-9786
Online: www.foxrunvineyards.com

At first sniff and sip, you will know you are onto something good here. For more than a century Fox Run was a dairy farm. The first grapes were planted in 1984, and the barn, erected shortly after the Civil War, was restored and opened as a winery in 1990 by Larry and Adele Wildrick. Three years later it was sold to Scott Osborn and investor Andy Hale, drawn to the property for its promise of fine winegrowing. With 60 acres of vines in production, Fox Run is one of the region's most influential enterprises, a testament to the ability of winemaker Peter Bell whose Rieslings are among the region's best. Don't miss Peter's Devonian Red, a blend of Cab Franc, Lemberger, and Merlot (named for a chapter in the region's geological history). In 2008, Fox Run was chosen as one of the top 100 wineries in the world by *Wine and Spirits Magazine.*

>Continue on Route 14 heading south, then turn left onto Randall Crossing Road.

MILES WINE CELLARS

168 Randall Crossing Road (off Route 14), Himrod, NY 14862
Phone: (607) 243-7742
Online: www.mileswinecellars.com

No winery in the Finger Lakes has more interesting history than Miles Wine Cellars. Originally a land-grant from the King of England to the Rapalee family, its dock on Seneca Lake provided area farmers with access to the barges that moved their produce to the big cities. The imposing house, built in 1802, was originally Federal-style in design, then converted to Greek Revival fifty years later. It became a stop on the "Underground Railroad," a shelter for runaway slaves as they made their way north and into Canada where they could live as free citizens. The Miles family purchased the Rapalee estate, unfazed by the local ghost stories, and developed a picture-book vineyard on part of the 115-acre property. As a respected grower, Doug Miles devotes full time to the grapevines, relinquishing winemaking to Peter Bell at nearby Fox Run. Besides tasting the

wines, you can sample small-batch ales made at the Abandon farmhouse brewery in Penn Yan, then stroll the surrounding lakefront grounds.
>*Get back onto Route 14 heading north to Geneva.*

BELHURST CASTLE 🍴 🛏

4069 Route 14 South, Geneva, NY 14456
Phone: (315) 781-0201
Online: www.belhurst.com
Dinner Hours: Daily, 5 PM to 9:30 PM

In 1885, Carrie Harron Collins, a wealthy descendant of Henry Clay of Kentucky, hired an architect and a crew of fifty laborers to begin work on a fairy-tale castle set amid twenty acres of forest on the shore of Seneca Lake. Four years later, Belhurst, the three-story, turreted, red-stone curiosity, was completed. The historic castle's gorgeous, over-the-top interior is an appropriate setting for Edgar's, not for the faint of heart when it comes to pushing carnivorous limits. The menu features Flat Iron, Porterhouse, and New York Strip Steaks, Filet Mignon, Roast Prime Ribs of Beef, Veal, Lamb, and Pork entrees. The sprawling Belhurst complex now includes two hotels. You can stay in the original castle chambers or the adjacent Vinifera Inn with king-size beds, Jacuzzis, gas fireplaces, and two -person showers. Listed on the National Register of Historic Places.

Entry Point:

CANANDAIGUA

(NORTH - WEST)

SCENIC & HISTORIC

WEEKEND TOUR

Friday

RHEINBLICK GERMAN RESTAURANT 🍴

224 S. Main Street, Canandaigua, NY 14424
Phone: (585) 905-0950
Online: www.rheinblick.hostei.com
Corkage Fee: none

The first wave of German immigrants arrived in Western New York in the mid-1800s, growing hops and honing beer brewing to a fine art. Dinner in the cozy dining room or at a table in the adjacent alley includes an impressive selection of German beers, both draft and bottled, to accompany schnitzels, wursts, bratens, and other pork, veal, and chicken entrées, along with starters and traditional sides like sauerkraut, egg noodles, and spätzle.

THE INN ON THE LAKE 🛏

770 South Main Street, Canandaigua, NY 14424
Phone: (800) 228-2801
Online: www.theinnonthelake.com

Perched at the edge of Canandaigua Lake's north shore, just a few steps from the Wine & Culinary Center. Request a room with lakefront patio or balcony, and bring a bathing suit for the indoor or outdoor pool. Good selection of local wines at either The Lounge or The Sand Bar, the seasonal poolside bar.

Saturday

LAFAYETTE RESTAURANT 🍴

408 Lakeshore Drive, Canandaigua, NY 14424
Phone: (585) 394-5383
Online: www.lafayettemotelandrestaurant.com

Breakfast at this 50-year-old local institution is a special pleasure. In a homey, diner-style setting, plates are piled high with eggs, waffles, pancakes, French toast, homemade breads, cinnamon buns, and fat pies. The staff is friendly and service is usually pretty quick. Take home a bag of house-blend coffee beans.

>*Drive west on Lakeshore Drive. Park along the lakefront near the Culinary Center.*

KERSHAW PARK 👪

A bedroom community for nearby Rochester and historically a popular summer retreat for wealthy city folk (Humphrey Bogart's family maintained a summertime cottage on the lake), Canandaigua was built on the site of a Seneca Indian village, becoming an important railroad junction and home port for several steamboats by the mid-19th century. Between 1920 and 1936, old cars among other things were dumped in the lake here to anchor the earth and rocks used to make the park. Stroll along the lakefront walkways or have an impromptu picnic at Kershaw Park, just off Lakeshore Drive, the original shoreline of the lake.

NEW YORK WINE & CULINARY CENTER 🛒

800 South Main Street, Canandaigua, NY 14424
Phone: (585) 394-7070
Online: www.nywcc.com

Keep walking. You're headed to the New York Wine & Culinary Center, northwest gateway to the bounty of food and wine produced throughout the state. The Center includes a demonstration theater, hands-on kitchen, bistro, gift boutique, and tasting room where you can acquaint yourself with wines and beers from around the state.

>*Drive north on Main Street; make a right onto Routes 5&20 heading east to Geneva.*

RED JACKET ORCHARDS 🛒

957 Routes 5&20, Geneva, NY 14456
Phone: (315) 781-2749
Online: www.redjacketorchards.com

Finger Lakes apples have a zest from the colder climate and high-acid soil, elevating malic acid, which gives the fruit its high-profile flavor. Red Jacket Orchards, in the hands of the Nicholson family since 1958, grows sixteen varieties of apples, including heirloom varieties that allow you to taste history. Try the Newton Pippins, a favorite of Benjamin Franklin. The farm store is stocked with a wide range of fruits, vegetables, jams, jellies, crackers and Amish goods.

>*Continue on Routes 5&20 heading east to into the city.*

GENEVA SOUTH MAIN STREET

Online: www.southmainst.com

Located at the northern outlet of Seneca Lake, the city was once a major village of the Seneca Nation, the tribe driven out during the punitive Sullivan Expedition of 1779. A walking tour starts at 380 South Main Street, the corner of William Street and South Main. The South Main Street Historic District extends from Seneca Street south to Conover Street, including 140 structures as well as Pulteney Park and the original quad of the Hobart College campus.

GENEVA HISTORICAL SOCIETY

543 South Main Street, Geneva, NY 14456
Phone: (315) 789-5151
Online: www.genevahistoricalsociety.com

Charles Butler, a Geneva attorney, built the Federal-style home in 1829. Phineas Prouty, a local merchant, purchased the home in 1842, and the property remained in the Prouty family for 60 years. Beverly Chew, the great-grandson of Phineas, then purchased the home in 1921, conveying the family residence to the Geneva Historical Society in 1960. The building houses the Geneva History Museum (exhibits are self-guided).

OPUS ESPRESSO AND WINE BAR

486 Exchange Street, Geneva, NY 14456
Phone: (315) 759-5388
Online: www.opusfingerlakes.com

Saturday Hours: 8 AM to 2 PM

This bouncy, obliging place has a joyfulness to it, offering well-crafted sustenance that speaks to the senses as well as the appetite. A selection of wines by the glass, half-glass, or bottle make this snug spot popular with nibblers and sippers. Service is expert and agile. If it's grab-and-go you have in mind, a server will fill your hamper with the makings of a first-rate picnic.

>*From downtown Geneva, drive back to Routes 5&20 heading west, then take Route 14 heading south; make a left turn onto Main Street in Dresden.*

ROBERT INGERSOLL BIRTHPLACE

61 Main Street, Dresden, NY 14441
Phone: (315) 536-1074
Online: www.rgimuseum.org

"There is no slavery but ignorance," said Robert Green Ingersoll, lawyer, Civil War veteran, political leader, and orator during the Golden Age of Freethought. His birthplace museum showcases Ingersoll's originality, his wit, his power as a persuader, and his role in history. Includes historical artifacts, displays, and a listening station invites visitors to hear three actual audio recordings of Ingersoll as recorded by Thomas Edison. (Open weekends during summer and fall).

>*Continue on Route 14 heading south; make a left turn onto Hansen Point Road.*

CLIMBING BINES

511 Hansen Point Road (just off Route 14), Penn Yan, NY 14527
Phone: (607) 745-0221
Online: www.climbingbineshopfarm.com

The stars have aligned at Climbing Bines, a hop farm and microbrewery, named for the vining plant that climbs by its shoots and wraps clockwise around its trellis, anchored on a farmstead settled by Chris Hansen's great-grandfather in 1905. Although most breweries don't have the real estate for growing their own ingredients, Chris, along with brewer Brian Karweck has developed a model farm-to-glass enterprise, utilizing 1500 estate-grown hop plants, a mix of 7 varieties, to lend flavors and aromas to a range of brews that are as distinctive and varied as those that grapes and soils give to wine. The "Pandemonium" beers (referencing an old name for Penn Yan in its less civilized past) use other local ingredients — barley, wheat, and rye — grown on nearby Peter Martin farm. The brewery's flagship Imperial IPA, made with earthy Cascade, Chinook and Nugget hops, stays true to the IPA's historical roots. Beers offered by the pint, in a flight, or in take-home growlers.

>*Continue on Route 14 heading south; make a left turn onto Randall Crossing Road.*

MILES WINE CELLARS

168 Randall Crossing Road (off Route 14), Himrod, NY 14862
Phone: (607) 243-7742
Online: www.mileswinecellars.com

This 200-year-old Greek Revival home, steeped in history, was once the site of a ferry crossing. It not only presides over a picture-book vineyard, but you can taste estate-grown wines in the "haunted" lakeside mansion. As an experienced and respected grower, Doug Miles devotes full time to the grapevines and relinquishes winemaking to Peter Bell at nearby Fox Run. Besides sipping wines, sample the small-batch ales made at the Abandon farmhouse brewery facility in Penn Yan, then stroll the surrounding waterfront grounds.

>*Continue on Route 14 heading south to the village of Watkins Glen; make a left turn onto Grandview Avenue and drive one block to Decatur Street.*

INTERNATIONAL MOTOR RACING RESEARCH CENTER

610 S. Decatur Street, Watkins Glen, NY 14891
Phone: (607) 535-9044
Online: www.racingarchives.org
Hours: Call for info

Watkins Glen is probably best known for its role in auto racing history; the first Watkins Glen Sports Car Grand Prix was held in 1948 on public streets around the village. Tucked away on a side street but worth finding, the International Motor Racing Research Center documents the heritage of amateur and professional motor racing, highlighting Sports Car, Formula 1, NASCAR, and vintage and Historic racing.

>*Get back onto Route 14 heading north. Just before the park entrance, turn left onto Route 329 (Old Corning Road), then right onto Walnut Road.*

SENECA LODGE

3600 Walnut Road, Watkins Glen, NY 14891
Phone: (607) 535-2014
Online: www.senecalodge.com
Hours: Bar opens at 4 PM

Swing open the wide, creaking door and walk through a wood-paneled dining room. Pull up a stool at one of the most unusual bars you will ever see. Since 1948, the Seneca Lodge Tavern Room has been a gathering place for the drivers and crews of the Grand Prix races. Behind the bar, laurel wreaths from the Formula 1 races of the 1970s hang from hundreds of arrows shot into the wall by archers who frequent the lodge for archery championships. Suspended from the ceiling are tires from NASCAR champions. House-brewed beers on tap include Blonde Ale, Belgian-style, and an agressively-hopped IPA.

>*Drive back to Route 14 heading north.*

GRAFT WINE & CIDER BAR

204 North Franklin Street (Route 14), Watkins Glen, NY 14891
Phone: (607) 210-4324
Online: www.facebook.com

Its name refers to the process of placing a shoot system of one grapevine species on the rootstock of another, not to political corruption in Albany. Sip local wines and ciders at the convivial bar, lined with a well of polished lake stones, or in one of the comfy benches; feast on creative, thoughtfully-prepared small plates, designed to share and pair by well-known local chefs Christina and Jonah McKeough.

WATKINS GLEN HARBOR HOTEL

16 North Franklin Street (Route 14), Watkins Glen, NY 14891
Phone: (607) 535-6116
Online: www.watkinsglenharborhotel.com

Nesting on the Southern-most point of Seneca Lake, hotel guestrooms are appointed with comfy pillow-topped mattresses covered with 310-thread count linens, plush duvet covers and feather pillows. Request a room with a view of the lake and enjoy a glass of local wine on your balcony.

Sunday

BLUE POINTE GRILLE

16 North Franklin Street (Route 14), Watkins Glen, NY 14891
Phone: (607) 535-6116
Online: www.watkinsglenharborhotel.com
Breakfast Hours: 7 AM to 11 AM

Start off your day with above-average hotel dining room breakfast fare, including omelets, made-to-order eggs, steak & eggs, cereals, waffles, French toast, pancakes, and coffee or espresso. Ask for a table on the lakeside patio and enjoy breakfast al fresco overlooking Seneca harbor.

WATKINS GLEN STATE PARK

You loved the pancakes. Now walk them off at the most famous of the Finger Lakes State Parks, with a reputation for leaving visitors spellbound. Within two miles, the glen's stream descends 400 feet past 200-foot cliffs, generating 19 waterfalls along its course. In 1933 President Franklin Roosevelt created the Civilian Conservation Corps in an effort to put unemployed men to work. They were responsible for building many of the present day pathways winding over and under waterfalls and through the spray of Cavern Cascade. The tunnels in the gorge were hand-cut in the rock. Wear comfortable shoes.

>Follow Route 414 (at 4th Street) heading north, along the eastern shore of Seneca Lake.

HAZLITT 1852 VINEYARDS ⚇

5712 Route 414, Hector, NY 14841
Phone: (607) 546-9463
Online: www.hazlitt1852.com

The 153 acres of fruit trees and vineyards purchased by David Hazlitt in 1852 has been tended by the Hazlitt family for six generations. The vineyards are situated on what is called Seneca Lake's "banana belt," consistently the warmest microclimate in the Finger Lakes as measured by Geneva Experiment Station thermometers, planted throughout the region. From Peach Orchard Point north to Lodi Point, the weather pattern keeps soil warmer into the fall. An extended growing season means the fruit has more time on the vine. With century-old Catawba grapevines and eight acres of Baco Noir on the property, one of the first wines produced by the winery was a proprietary blend of the two. Combining both of these early-ripening, high-acid varieties proved much better than either one on its own, especially with added sugar for balance. The popularity of "Red Cat" has been explained as a beginning drinker's bridge between Coca-Cola and more serious wines.

STANDING STONE VINEYARDS ⚇

9934 Route 414, Hector, NY 14841
Phone: (607) 582-6051
Online: www.standingstonewines.com

These are vineyards with a pedigree. First planted by Charles Fournier and Guy DeVeaux of Gold Seal Winery as "Area 13," they represent some of the oldest vinifera plantings in the region. Notable is the North Block Riesling with fruit sourced from the historic vines. Standing Stone (the name inspired by native Indian legend), established in 1991 by Tom and Marti Macinski, has made a name for itself with ice wines. If you have never had the opportunity to try one of these remarkable dessert wines, here's the place to do it.

DAÑO'S ON SENECA ⚇

9564 Route 414, Lodi, NY
Phone: (607) 582-7555
Online: www.danosonseneca.com

Hours: 12 Noon to 9 PM
Corkage Fee: $15

You brush past the chef's herb garden and peer into his kitchen as you enter the restaurant. Daño Hutnik is a superb chef who has played a major role in making the Finger Lakes a food as well as a wine region. The stage of his Austrian wine garden-inspired eatery features sleek counters stacked with pastries and filled with platters of rustic salads and main dishes. Daño's on Seneca is a Finger Lakes translation of the convivial roadside taverns (heurigers) in the wine-growing regions around Vienna. Servers help you assemble a meal to suit your appetite which you can enjoy inside the charming space or on an open-air patio with a view of the lake. Sip the house wine served in glass mugs (viertels) and forget the cares of the world.

WAGNER VINEYARDS

9322 Route 414, Lodi, NY 14860
Phone: (607) 582-6450
Online: www.wagnervineyards.com

If the Finger Lakes were a dartboard, Wagner Vineyards would most likely be its bulls-eye, equidistant from all corners of the region – rather fitting, since this enterprise played a central role in the early growth and development of the region's wine industry. Bill Wagner's vision was to create wines that belong in the company of the great wines of the world. By almost any measure, he succeeded in making that vision a reality. His octagonal building is a Finger Lakes landmark. The winery produces a total of thirty wines, all from the estate's 240 acres of vineyards, and all over the varietal map. Focus is on the award-winning Rieslings — dry, semi-dry, sweet, sparkling, and ice wines (many with practical screw caps). The adjacent microbrewery offers six standard brews in addition to seasonal specialties.

>Continue on Route 414 heading north to Route 96A.

EREMITA WINERY

2155 East Church Street (at Routes 414 & 96A), Lodi NY 14860
Phone: (607) 474-5002

Online: www.eremitawinery.com

In 1799, the village of Lodi was settled by Dutch farmers from New Jersey who formed a Dutch Reformed community. In July of 1872, after their church burned, the congregation began building a new church, dedicated July 15, 1873, and for many years the church was shared by both Dutch Reformed and Presbyterian congregations. Light still streams in through stained glass windows, but the pews are gone, and the altar has been replaced by a circular bar salvaged from a tavern in Medina. Stop for a visit, if only to sip the bone-dry Riesling in one of the most unusual tasting rooms in the region.

>In Ovid, Routes 414 & 96A split; turn left and continue on Route 96A to Geneva.

ROSE HILL MANSION

3373 Route 96A (just south of Routes 5&20), Geneva, NY 14456
Phone: (315) 789-3848
Online: www.rosehillmansion.com
Sunday Hours: 1 PM to 5 PM (call for tour information)

One of the finest examples of the Greek Revival Style in the United States, Rose Hill was built in 1837 on a military tract granted to Revolutionary War soldiers. Its monumental scale reflects the prosperity of Western New York as a result of the Erie Canal. The property was declared a National Historic Landmark in 1986.

>Drive north on Route 96A to Route 5&20 heading west, then take Route 14 heading south.

GENEVA ON THE LAKE

1001 Lochland Road (Route 14), Geneva, NY 14456
Phone: (315) 789-7190
Online: www.genevaonthelake.com

One of the genuine icons of the Finger Lakes. Built in 1914 as a private home and modeled after the Lancelotti villa in the hills of Frascati near Rome, its interior includes Italian marble fireplaces, tapestries, Ionic columns and wood-coffered ceilings. The villa later became a monastery, and then, in 1981, a boutique hotel, managed with impeccable expertise by Bill Schickel. The Lancellotti Dining Room provides a courtly setting for candlelight dinner (local wine-pairing flight available). Flaming desserts served tableside. The mood brightens in summer when the doors are thrown open for patio dining. After a stroll amid spectacular lakeside gardens and classical sculptures, settle in to one of the suites or studios appointed with Stickley furniture. The period atmosphere evokes a gentler time, and it is very easy to get lost in the moment here.

Entry Point:

HAMMONDSPORT

(SOUTH - WEST)

SCENIC & HISTORIC

DAY TRIP

KEUKA ARTISAN BAKERY & DELI ✍️

49 Shethar Street, Hammondsport, NY 14840
Phone: (607) 224-4001
Online: www.keukaartisanbakery.com
Breakfast Hours: 7 AM to 11 AM

Just steps from the village square, the aroma of fresh-baked breads and sweets will stop you in your tracks. The breads enclose breakfast sandwiches and are toasted to accompany omelets-of-the-day. Save room for dessert from the pastry counter with locally-roasted coffee or espresso, and don't forget to take along a warm-out-of-the oven baguette to support your day of touring.

PULTENEY SQUARE HISTORIC DISTRICT 🔭

Picturesque Hammondsport, on the South end of the lake, has a long history as a vintner's enclave. The first wine grapes in the Finger Lakes were cultivated here in 1829 by William Bostwick, minister of St. James Episcopal Church, and commercial wine production began here in 1860. The district includes 15 buildings clustered around Pulteney Square, a village green with a turn-of-the-century bandstand. The square was named for Sir William Pulteney, the wealthiest man in late 18th century Great Britain, who invested in America by purchasing one million acres of land in western New York State.

>*Take Route 54A (Pulteney Street) heading north out of the village, then bear left onto G. H. Taylor Memorial Drive.*

BULLY HILL VINEYARDS 🍷

8843 G. H. Taylor Memorial Drive, Hammondsport, NY 14840
Phone: (607) 868-3610
Online: www.bullyhill.com

Bully Hill's founder, Walter Taylor, was a larger-than-life character in a sweeping epic of Finger Lakes Wine Country. The grandson of the founder of the Taylor Wine Company and an eager provocateur, Walter railed against the "wine factory" the company had become by the time it was swallowed up by Coca-Cola in 1977. He was a marketing genius whose sense of humor provided an antidote to wine snobbery. While the rascally, holy-terror personality of Walter Taylor is gone from his beloved winery, his anti-establishment wine making and off-the-wall labels have earned him a hero's status in the Finger Lakes. Visit here, if only to soak up a bit of the lore of the legendary "Baron of Bully Hill."

GREYTON H. TAYLOR WINE MUSEUM 📛

Greyton H. Taylor Memorial Drive, Hammondsport, NY 14840
Phone: (607) 868-4814
Online: www.bullyhill.com/museum/museum.asp
Hours: Monday thru Saturday, 10 AM to 5 PM; Sunday, 11:30 AM to 5 PM (mid-May thru October)

On the grounds of Bully Hill Vineyards, the first wine museum in America is devoted to the Taylor family endeavor that began in 1878. The Cooper Shop Building includes local memorabilia and wine making equipment from the early days of the Finger Lakes wine industry. The Art Gallery houses original artwork by Walter S. Taylor artifacts from the days of Prohibition, presidential glassware, and a collection of Taylor family photos.

>Take Sanford Road to Route 76. Turn left, heading north.

HERON HILL WINERY 🍷

9301 County Route 76, Hammondsport, NY 14840
Phone: (800) 441-4241
Online: www.heronhill.com

What began as the 1977 grapegrowing endeavor of John and Josephine Ford Ingle (she is the great-granddaughter of Henry Ford) has become one of the region's most prominent wineries. In 2000, the winery was transformed into an architecturally flamboyant, state-of-the-art facility, a postmodern edifice with rounded, vaulted ceilings suggestive of a giant wine barrel. With some of the area's most impressive views of the vineyards and Keuka Lake, Heron Hill was chosen as one of the ten most spectacular tasting rooms in the world by *Travel + Leisure.* The winemaking team is led by Bernard Cannac who studied Enology at the University of Bordeaux and the Ecole Superieure de Commerce de Dijon. Among the portfolio of nearly 20 varieties, most noteworthy are Rieslings from the family

-farmed Ingle Vineyard.

>*Continue north on Route 76, then bear right onto Middle Road.*

DR. FRANK'S VINIFERA WINE CELLARS

9749 Middle Road, Hammondsport, NY 14840
Phone: (800) 320-0735
Online: www.drfrankwines.com

The Frank family is the closest we have to royalty in the Finger Lakes. Fred, president and general manager is now entrusted to preserve the historical accomplishments of his grandfather, Konstantin Frank, the Ukrainian-born doctor of enology who is credited with changing the course of wine growing in the Finger Lakes. *Wine Report* named Dr. Frank Cellars the "Greatest Wine Producer in the Northeast." In the 1950s, Dr. Frank planted an old, winter-hardy, German Riesling clone, prized for its low yields of intensely aromatic and flavorful fruit with classic mineral notes, and the wines here behave as German Rieslings typically do. Not only are they deliciously vivacious in their youth, they continue drinking well as they become complex and more-nuanced with age. Willy Frank, Fred's father, called the older Rieslings his "Marlene Dietrich wines." You may end up drinking some of the best wines on the planet here, and in surely one of the prettiest places it's grown.

>*Continue heading north on Middle Road, make a right turn onto Shuart Road, then a left onto Route 54A heading north along the western shore of Keuka Lake (about 20 minutes).*

ESPERANZA MANSION

3456 Route 54-A, Bluff Point, NY 14478
Phone: (315) 536-4400
Online: www.esperanzamansion.com
Hours: Call for seasonal schedule
Corkage Fee: $15

John Nicholas Rose, the son of Robert and Jane Rose, journeyed to the Finger Lakes region from the family plantation in Stafford County, Virginia. He purchased 1,000 acres of land and completed construction of the home he called "Esperanza" (derived from the Latin word for "hope") in 1838. It's a little piece of heaven sitting astride the Keuka highlands — a Greek Revival mansion fully renovated to its 19th century splendor. Offering three separate dining areas, outdoor terrace and patio seating with a breathtaking view. Put on your sunglasses and grab an outdoor seat. Among the dazzling vistas along Keuka Lake, this place may be the best.

>*Return to Hammondsport on Route 54A, then make a right turn onto Route 54 heading south.*

GLENN H. CURTISS AVIATION MUSEUM

8419 Route 54, Hammondsport, NY 14840-9795
Phone: (607) 569-2160
Online: www.glennhcurtissmuseum.org

Born in Hammondsport in 1878, Glenn Curtiss made innumerable contributions to early aviation, producing and selling the first private airplane, receiving pilot's license #1, design and construction of the first successful pontoon aircraft in America, invention of dual pilot control, and design of retractable landing gear. A glimpse into local aviation history, the museum houses a full-scale reproduction of the first naval aircraft as well as a 1912 "Pusher," a 1913 "Model E" flying boat, a 1917 "Jenny," a 1919 "Seagull" flying boat, and a 1927 "Robin," as well as displays, exhibits, and interactive gallery relating to local winemaking and turn of-the-century life. (Admission: Adults $8.50; Seniors $7; Students $5.50; Kids free)

>*Drive north on Route 54, make a left turn onto Route 54A, then another left onto Lake Street (which becomes Pleasant Valley Road).*

PLEASANT VALLEY WINE COMPANY

8260 Pleasant Valley Road, Hammondsport, NY 14840
Phone: (607) 569-6111
Online: www.pleasantvalleywine.com

The past is prologue, so an understanding of Finger Lakes wine culture wouldn't be complete without a visit here. The Pleasant Valley Wine Company is now home to the Great Western, Gold Seal, and Widmer brands, once mighty giants in the wine industry. The 25-minute tour includes a bus ride to the original 1860 Great Western facility (Bonded Winery No. 1) and a display of artifacts from early winemaking in the region. Even the wines are museum pieces, most made with native variety grapes, now out of favor as drinkers become more sophisticated in their taste preferences.

>Return to the village, turn left onto Main Street (Route 54A), following right onto Pulteney Street. Drive to the corner of Mechanic Street.

THE VILLAGE TAVERN

30 Mechanic Street, Hammondsport, NY 14840
Phone: (607) 569-2528
Online: www.villagetaverninn.com
Hours: Daily, 5 PM to 9 PM (Memorial Day to October 31); Call for off-season schedule
Corkage Policy: No outside wine allowed

Winery folks have made the Village Tavern their central gathering place, but anyone feels welcome. Careful not to drop the wine list on your foot, as you could really hurt yourself. One of the thrills of eating here is the opportunity to browse through the encyclopedic, all-Finger Lakes wine list, novel for both its breadth and entertainment value. Ambitious dinner menu offers a bit of something for everyone.

KEUKA LAKESIDE INN

24 Water Street, Hammondsport, NY 14840
Phone: (607) 569-2600
Online: www.keukalakesideinn.com

It's all about the view at this updated, old-style motel perched at the water's edge and just a short walk from the village square. At the end of the day, relax in the gazebo and contemplate the serene waters of Keuka, the name the Seneca people gave to the lake for their "canoe landing."

Entry Point:

HAMMONDSPORT

(SOUTH - WEST)

SCENIC & HISTORIC

WEEKEND TOUR

Friday

THE VILLAGE TAVERN 🍴

30 Mechanic Street, Hammondsport, NY 14840
Phone: (607) 569-2528
Online: www.villagetaverninn.com
Hours: 5 PM to 9 PM
Corkage Policy: No outside wine allowed

Winery folks have made the Village Tavern their central gathering place, but anyone feels welcome. Careful not to drop the wine list on your foot, as you could really hurt yourself. One of the thrills of eating here is the opportunity to browse through the encyclopedic, all-Finger Lakes wine list, novel for both its breadth and entertainment value. Ambitious dinner menu offers a bit of something for everyone.

KEUKA LAKESIDE INN 🛏️

24 Water Street, Hammondsport, NY 14840
Phone: (607) 569-2600
Online: www.keukalakesideinn.com

It's all about the view at this updated, old-style motel perched at the water's edge and just a short walk from the village square. At the end of the day, relax in the gazebo and contemplate the serene waters of Keuka, the name the Seneca people gave to the lake, meaning "Canoe Landing."

Saturday

KEUKA ARTISAN BAKERY & DELI 🍴

49 Shethar Street, Hammondsport, NY 14840
Phone: (607) 224-4001
Online: www.keukaartisanbakery.com
Breakfast Hours: 7 AM to 11 AM

Just steps from the village square, the aroma of fresh-baked breads and sweets will stop you in your tracks. The breads enclose breakfast sandwiches and are toasted to accompany omelets-of-the-day. Save room for dessert from the pastry counter with locally-roasted coffee or espresso, and don't forget to take along a baguette to support your day of touring.

PULTENEY SQUARE

Picturesque Hammondsport, on the South end of the lake, has a long history as a vintner's enclave. The first wine grapes in the Finger Lakes were cultivated here in 1829 by William Bostwick, minister of St. James Episcopal Church, and commercial wine production began here in 1860. The district includes 15 buildings clustered around Pulteney Square, a village green with a turn-of-the-century bandstand. The square was named for Sir William Pulteney, the wealthiest man in late 18th century Great Britain, who invested in America by purchasing one million acres of land in western New York State.

>*From Pulteney Street, turn left onto Main Street, then right onto Lake Street (which becomes Pleasant Valley Road).*

PLEASANT VALLEY WINE COMPANY

8260 Pleasant Valley Road, Hammondsport, NY 14840
Phone: (607) 569-6111
Online: www.pleasantvalleywine.com

The past is prologue, so an understanding of Finger Lakes wine culture wouldn't be complete without a visit here. The Pleasant Valley Wine Company is now home to the Great Western, Gold Seal, and Widmer brands, once mighty giants in the wine industry. The 25-minute tour includes a bus ride to the original 1860 Great Western facility (Bonded Winery No. 1) and a display of artifacts from early winemaking in the region. Even the wines are museum pieces, most made with native varie-ty grapes, now out of favor as drinkers become more sophisticated in their taste preferences.

>*Return to the village, turn left onto Main Street (Route 54A), following to Pulteney Street heading north out of the village, then bear left onto G. H. Taylor Memorial Drive.*

BULLY HILL VINEYARDS 🍷

8843 G. H. Taylor Memorial Drive, Hammondsport, NY 14840
Phone: (607) 868-3610
Online: www.bullyhill.com

Bully Hill's founder, Walter Taylor, was a larger-than-life character in a sweeping epic of Finger Lakes Wine Country. The grandson of the founder of the Taylor Wine Company and an eager provocateur, Walter railed against the "wine factory" the company had become by the time it was swallowed up by Coca-Cola in 1977. He was a marketing genius whose sense of humor provided an antidote to wine snobbery. While the rascally, holy-terror personality of Walter Taylor is gone from his beloved winery, his anti-establishment wine making and off-the-wall labels have earned him a hero's status in the Finger Lakes. Visit here, if only to soak up a bit of the lore of the legendary "Baron of Bully Hill."

GREYTON H. TAYLOR WINE MUSEUM

Greyton H. Taylor Memorial Drive, Hammondsport, NY 14840
Phone: (607) 868-4814
Online: www.bullyhill.com/museum/museum.asp
Hours: 10 AM to 5 PM

On the grounds of Bully Hill Vineyards, the first wine museum in America is devoted to the Taylor family endeavor that began in 1878. The Cooper Shop Building includes local memorabilia and wine making equipment from the early days of the Finger Lakes wine industry. The Art Gallery houses original artwork by Walter S. Taylor artifacts from the days of Prohibition, presidential glassware, and a collection of Taylor family photos.

>Take Sanford Road to Route 76. Turn left, heading north.

HERON HILL WINERY 🍷

9301 County Route 76, Hammondsport, NY 14840
Phone: (800) 441-4241
Online: www.heronhill.com

What began as the 1977 grapegrowing endeavor of John and Josephine Ford Ingle (she is the great-granddaughter of Henry Ford) has become one of the region's most prominent wineries. In 2000, the winery was transformed into an architecturally flamboyant, state-of-the-art facility, a postmodern edifice with rounded, vaulted ceilings suggestive of a giant wine barrel. With some of the area's most impressive views of the vineyards and Keuka Lake, Heron Hill was chosen as one of the ten most spectacular tasting rooms in the world by *Travel + Leisure*. The winemaking team is led by Bernard Cannac who studied Enology at the University of Bordeaux and the Ecole Superieure de Commerce de Dijon. Among the portfolio of nearly 20 varieties, most noteworthy are Rieslings from the family-farmed Ingle Vineyard.

>*Continue north on Route 76, then bear right onto Middle Road.*

DR. FRANK'S VINIFERA WINE CELLARS 🍷

9749 Middle Road, Hammondsport, NY 14840
Phone: (800) 320-0735
Online: www.drfrankwines.com

The Frank family is the closest we have to royalty in the Finger Lakes. Fred, president and general manager is now entrusted to preserve the historical accomplishments of his grandfather, Konstantin Frank, the Ukrainian-born doctor of enology who is credited with changing the course of wine growing in the Finger Lakes. *Wine Report* named Dr. Frank Cellars the "Greatest Wine Producer in the Northeast." In the 1950s, Dr. Frank planted an old, winter-hardy, German Riesling clone, prized for its low yields of intensely aromatic and flavorful fruit with classic mineral notes, and the wines here behave as German Rieslings typically do. Not only are they deliciously vivacious in their youth, they continue drinking well as they become complex and more-nuanced with age. Willy Frank, Fred's father, called the older Rieslings his "Marlene Dietrich wines." You may end up drinking some of the best wines on the planet here, and in surely one of the prettiest places it's grown.

>*Continue heading north on Middle Road, make a right turn onto Shuart Road, then a left onto Route 54A heading north along the western shore of the lake (about 15 minutes). Make a left turn onto Italy Hill Road.*

HUNT COUNTRY VINEYARDS ⚛

4021 Italy Hill Road, Branchport, NY 14418
Phone: (315) 595-2812
Online: www.huntcountryvineyards.com

The vineyards encompass 50 acres of well-tended grapes, crafted into exceptional wines including Chardonnay, Pinot Gris, Cabernet Franc, and Rieslings. But what excels here is the art of sculpting frozen fruit into ice wines, so good they have accompanied dessert at White House dinners. Hardy Vignoles grapes are left on the vines past traditional harvest time so more sugar and interesting characters can develop. When temperatures drop to 20 degrees or below, they are picked by hand, carried to the winery, and pressed immediately, as juice is separated from skin and pulp, drop by drop. They produce a wonderful dessert wine with mouth-filling texture and hints of apricots and tropical fruit. Expect to pay dearly for ice wines, but they are well worth the splurge.

>Get back onto Route 54A heading north to Bluff Point.

ESPERANZA MANSION 🍴

3456 Route 54-A, Bluff Point, NY 14478
Phone: (315) 536-4400
Online: www.esperanzamansion.com
Hours: Call for seasonal schedule
Corkage Fee: $15

John Nicholas Rose, the son of Robert and Jane Rose, journeyed to the Finger Lakes region from the family plantation in Stafford County, Virginia. He purchased 1,000 acres of land and completed construction of the home he called "Esperanza" (derived from the Latin word for "hope") in 1838. It's a little piece of heaven sitting astride the Keuka highlands — a Greek Revival mansion fully renovated to its 19th century splendor. Offering three separate dining areas, outdoor terrace and patio seating with a breathtaking view. Put on your sunglasses and grab an outdoor seat. Among dazzling vistas along Keuka Lake, this place may be the best.

>From Route 54A, turn right onto Pepper Road and drive to Skyline Drive (about 10 minutes).

GARRETT CHAPEL

5251 Skyline Drive, Bluff Point, NY 14478
Phone: (315) 536-3955
Hours: Sunrise to Sunset (March thru October)
Online: www.garrettchapel.org

It has history, it has wine country significance, and it has a tragic story. Constructed in the Norman Gothic style and known as the "Little Chapel on the Mount," the chapel was commissioned by Evelyn and Paul Garrett who ran Garrett and Company (once among the largest wine producers in the world), mourning the death of their son Charles who died of tuberculosis in 1929. The chapel was deeded to the Episcopal Diocese of Rochester in 1931.

>Return to Route 54A heading north to the village of Penn Yan.

YATES COUNTY HISTORY CENTER

107 Chapel Street, Penn Yan, NY 14527
Phone: (315) 536-7318
Online: www.yatespast.org

Stop by for a peek into the past. Just off Main Street, this "public history museum" features the vast collection of L. Caroline Underwood, a local teacher and passionate supporter of local history. A carriage house behind the museum is home to an exhibit of the life of Jemima Wilkinson, one of the first female visionaries of religion and Women's rights. Jemima and her group of followers, the Society of Universal Friends, formed the first pioneer settlement in what is presently Yates County. Consisting of almost 300 members in 1790, they and their followers were the first white people that the Native Americans in this region ever saw. (Saturday hours by appointment).

KEUKA RESTAURANT

12 Main Street, Penn Yan, NY 14527
Phone: (315) 536-5852
Online: www.keuka-restaurant.com
Hours: 11 AM to 10 PM
Corkage Fee: $8

You don't come to Penn Yan expecting molecular gastronomy. The food is conservative, small-town, American family restaurant fare – sandwiches, burgers, steaks, ribs, fish fry — nothing fancy, but it's done properly. The menu offers a range of local wines and beers.

SENECA FARMS ICE CREAM

2485 Route 54A, Penn Yan, NY 14527
Phone: (315) 536-4066
Online: www.senecafarmsny.com

When in Penn Yan, do as the locals do. After dinner drive over to this 1950s-era ice cream parlor for a Turtle Sundae with homemade vanilla ice cream, hot fudge and hot caramel sauces, and toasted pecans. (Open March thru end of October)

BEST WESTERN VINEYARD INN & SUITES

142 Lake Street, Penn Yan, NY 14527
Phone: (315) 536-8473
Online: www.vineyardinnandsuites.com

Clean, comfortable, up-to-date accommodations within walking distance to downtown with fitness center, indoor heated pool, hot tub and business center. Rooms have a mini-fridge for the wine you purchased earlier in the day.

Sunday

PENN YAN DINER

131 East Elm Street, Penn Yan, NY 14527
Phone: (315) 536-6004
Online: www.pennyandiner.com

Breakfast here isn't anything you can't get most elsewhere, except for the sense of small town charm and the fact that you get to eat in a real diner. It's a genuine slice of Americana, built in 1925 by the Richardson Dining Car factory, the first diner manufacturer in western New York, and it's had a succession of owners over the years, operated since 2012 by Carrie and Sean Ahearn. Freshly-brewed Finger Lakes Coffee Roasters' beans make a damn good cup of coffee.

PENN YAN HISTORIC DISTRICT

The name of the village was contrived from the first syllables of "Pennsylvania" and "Yankee," as most of the early settlers were Pennsylvanians and New Englanders (or Yankees). After breakfast at the diner, do some exploring on foot. Stroll over to the historic district with a broad range of architecturally significant examples of residential, commercial, industrial, civic and ecclesiastical structures. Highlights include the Birkett Mills, Chronicle Building, Knapp Hotel, and the Castner House.

>From Main Street, turn right onto Lake Street (Route 54) heading south.

RED JACKET PARK

The small lakefront park, named for the Native American chief of the Seneca tribe to whom President George Washington presented a "peace medal," features a statue in his honor. The pebbly beach is one of the best public beaches in the region, extremely clean and the water tends to be very calm.

>Continue on Route 54 heading south along the eastern shore of Keuka Lake.

KEUKA HOTEL

As you drive along Route 54, you pass the (unmarked) site of the old Keuka Hotel near the foot of Hyatt Hill in the town of Wayne (named in honor of Revolutionary War hero General Anthony Wayne), built on the lakeshore by James Washburn in 1894 and demolished in 1974. Rudyard Kipling and Arthur Conan Doyle were both early guests of the hotel. Hoagy Carmichael was the pianist and vocalist in the hotel ballroom during the 1926 and 1927 seasons, and local legend has it that he wrote "Stardust," one of the most recorded songs of the 20th century, during his time at the hotel.

>*Continue on Route 54 heading south (about 15 minutes). Turn left onto Hyatt Hill Road, then left onto Dutch Street.*

MCGREGOR VINEYARD WINERY ⊻

5503 Dutch Street, Dundee, NY 14837
Phone: (607) 292-3999
Online: www.mcgregorwinery.com

One of Keuka Lake's most venerable producers, the rustic winery, vineyards and adjoining picnic grounds attract visitors to this 1,200-foot perch overlooking Bluff Point at the widest expanse of Keuka Lake. The combination of cool temperatures and significant "lake effect" winds on the steep, north-facing slope stresses the vines, produces smaller yields, and results in more mature and concentrated flavors in the grapes. Semisweet Riesling is a long-standing success story, and the winery makes its mark on Finger Lakes viticulture with plantings of rare, Eastern-European wine grapes, propagated from a mother lode of cuttings that originated in the former Soviet Republic of Georgia. Two hardy varieties with noble bloodlines, Saperavi and Sereksia Charni, are married to produce an audacious red wine called "Black Russian."

>*Get back onto Route 54 heading south and watch for Switzerland Inn on the right.*

SWITZERLAND INN 🍴

14109 Keuka Village Road (Route 54), Hammondsport, NY 14840
Phone: (607) 292-6927
Online: www.theswitz.com
Corkage Fee: $10

This sprawling, multi-level old dame shows her age in places. Hugging the eastern shore of Keuka Lake, "the Switz" has been in continuous operation since 1894. Ask for a table on the deck overlooking the lake, and order from a menu of soups, salads, burgers, sandwiches, pizza, and fish fry.

>*Continue on Route 54 heading south.*

GLENN H. CURTISS AVIATION MUSEUM

8419 Route 54, Hammondsport, NY 14840
Phone: (607) 569-2160
Online: www.glennhcurtissmuseum.org

Born in Hammondsport in 1878, Glenn Curtiss made innumerable contributions to early aviation, producing and selling the first private airplane, receiving pilot's license #1, design and construction of the first successful pontoon aircraft in America, invention of dual pilot control, and design of retractable landing gear. A glimpse into local aviation history, the museum houses a full-scale reproduction of the first naval aircraft as well as a 1912 "Pusher," a 1913 "Model E" flying boat, a 1917 "Jenny," a 1919 "Seagull" flying boat, and a 1927 "Robin," as well as displays, exhibits, and interactive gallery relating to local winemaking and turn of-the-century life. (Admission: Adults $8.50; Seniors $7; Students $5.50; Kids free)

>*Follow Route 54 to Route 415 heading south to Corning (about 30 minutes).*

CORNING MUSEUM OF GLASS

1 Museum Way, Corning, NY 14830
Phone: (800) 732-6845
Online: www.cmog.org
Hours: 9 AM to 5 PM (Extended summer hours until 8 PM)

The Bay State Glass Company was established in Somerville, Massachusetts, in 1851 by Amory Houghton and became Corning Glass Works when it moved to this picturesque city in 1868. Opened in 1951, the company's 100th anniversary, the Corning Museum of Glass is a not-for-profit home to the world's most comprehensive showcase of glass, including more than 50,000 pieces of glass art, some dating from 1500 B.C. You may explore the science and technology of glass in a hands-on exhibit area, see live narrated glassmaking demonstrations, and try your own hand at glassworking. (Admission: Adults $15; Seniors $12; Kids & Teens free)

ROCKWELL MUSEUM OF WESTERN ART

111 Cedar Street, Corning, NY 14830
Phone: (607) 937-5386

Online: www.rockwellmuseum.org

Hours: 9 AM to 5 PM (Extended summer hours until 8 PM)

The finest collection of Western and Native American art in the East, rotating a permanent collection of art through galleries based on themes: Wilderness, Buffalo, Horse, Indian and Cowboy. (Admission: Adults $8; Seniors $7; Students $7)

MARKET STREET BREWING COMPANY

63 West Market Street, Corning, NY 14830

Phone: (607) 936-2337

Online: www.936-beer.com

Corkage Fee: $5

Stroll along historic Market Street in what Rand-McNally called "the Most Fun Small Town in America," then settle in for dinner at Pelham and Theresa McClellan's beer-centered eatery. The ambitious brewpub offers house-brewed beers, from the lighter Mad Bug Lager to the more robust English-style D'Artagnan Dark Ale, along with dishes like beer-braised bratwurst served with a side of honey-beer mustard. Weather permitting, alfresco dining available in the "biergarten."

RADISSON HOTEL CORNING

125 Denison Parkway East, Corning, NY 14830

Phone: (607) 962-5000

Online: www.radisson.com/corning

Located in Corning's Gaffer District and convenient to the Corning Museum of Glass, the smoke-free and pet-friendly Radisson has an indoor pool and fitness center; all rooms include free Wi-Fi Internet access, large work desk, ergonomic chairs, flat-screen TV and room service from the hotel restaurant. Local wine selections available at the Steuben Bar, located off the lobby.

Entry Point:

ITHACA

(SOUTH - EAST)

SCENIC & HISTORIC

DAY TRIP

STATE DINER

428 West State Street, Ithaca, NY 14850
Phone: (607) 272-6189
Online: www.thestatediner.com

Slide into a booth at this artifact of Ithaca's culinary culture, a bona fide Greek diner that has served local citizens of all ages, nationalities and walks of life since 1936. There's nothing quite like a diner breakfast, with its steaming cups of coffee, formica countertop, and plates of eggs and crisp bacon.

>*Take Buffalo Street heading up East Hill, then turn left onto Stewart Avenue and continue to the Cornell campus.*

CORNELL UNIVERSITY

Consistently ranked among the top 20 universities in the world, Cornell sits on a hilltop overlooking 40-mile-long Cayuga Lake and teems with intellectual energy. Two sides of the campus are bound by gorges, cut during the last 12,000 years. Creeks and waterfalls fill the gorges, and no matter where you are on campus you are never far from the sight and sound of falling water. A quiet Saturday morning is a good time to visit. Pick up the morning paper at Willard Straight Hall and stroll along the historic Arts Quad where you'll hear the ring of chimes from McGraw Tower played by student chimemasters every 15 minutes a day during the school year (with a reduced number of performances when classes are not in session).

HERBERT F. JOHNSON MUSEUM OF ART

114 Central Avenue (Cornell Campus), Ithaca, NY 14853
Hours: Tuesday thru Sunday, 10 AM to 5 PM (Closed Monday)
Online: www.museum.cornell.edu

This is your day for serious art appreciation. Built on the crest of Cornell's Library Slope, the very spot where Ezra Cornell determined the location for his university, the Johnson Museum is a work of art itself, designed by master of modern architecture I.M. Pei. Spanning the history of art, with special strengths in Asian art, 19th- and 20th-century American art, and the graphic arts, the museum houses more than 35,000 works of art in its permanent collection, including works by William Hogarth, Francisco Goya, Édouard Manet, Charles-François Daubigny, Edgar Degas, Henri de Toulouse-Lautrec, and Henri Matisse. There are also extensive holdings of American artists, including Georgia O'Keeffe and Andy Warhol. The view from the top floor of the Museum is one of the best in all of the Finger Lakes. The main pedestrian access is from the Arts Quad to the east.

SUSPENSION BRIDGE 👀

Just across University Avenue from the museum, the pedestrian bridge, built in 1960, crosses 138 feet above Fall Creek, connecting students who live on North Campus to Central Campus. According to Cornell legend, if a couple crosses the suspension bridge and the young woman does not accept a kiss from her partner, the bridge will collapse into the gorge. If the kiss is accepted, the couple is assured a long future together.

>*Take College Avenue to State Street heading downtown.*

THE HISTORY CENTER 👀

401 East State/MLK Jr. Street, Ithaca, NY 14850
Phone: (607) 273-8284
Hours: Tuesday, Thursday and Saturday, 11 AM to 5 PM (and by appointment)
Online: www.thehistorycenter.net

Wend back into town for a visit to the History Center and get to know what makes the city tick. Explore Ithaca and Tompkins County through beautifully curated museum exhibits and a research library for casual readers and scholars, school children, local historians, genealogists, and professional researchers.

>*Drive across downtown to Route 13 North.*

ITHACA BAKERY 🍴 🛒

400 North Meadow Street (Route 13 North), Ithaca, NY 14850
Phone: (607) 273-7110
Online: www.ithacabakery.com

Hobnob with the locals at Ithaca Bakery. This culinary landmark has supplied Ithaca with fresh-baked bread since 1902, and what better use for that bread than for a menu of "outrageous" sandwiches. A glass display case is loaded with salads and side dishes (take along the makings of a picnic at Stewart Park).

>*Follow Route 13 heading north and take exit to Route 34. Make a left turn onto Route 34, then an immediate left to the park entrance.*

STEWART PARK 🔭

It was once the site of Wharton Brothers Studio, where Theodore and Leopold Wharton produced over 100 silent films from 1914 through 1919, an era when moviemaking was an emerging art form and burgeoning industry. (Ray June, a native Ithacan and graduate of Cornell, worked for the Whartons before becoming a cinematographer at MGM. He was director of photography for such films as *Horse Feathers* with the Marx Brothers and *Funny Face*, starring Fred Astaire and Audrey Hepburn). Today the lakeside municipal park offers several facilities including tennis courts, playground with play structures including carousel, athletic fields, duck pond, spray pool, municipal golf course, and bird sanctuary.

>*Leaving the park, take a right turn to Route 13 South. Make a left turn onto 3rd Street, then an immediate left onto Franklin Street and continue to 1st Street.*

SCIENCECENTER 🔭

601 1st Street, Ithaca, NY 14850
Phone: (607) 272-0600
Online: www.sciencenter.org
Hours: Tuesday thru Saturday, 10 AM to 5 PM: Sunday, 12 Noon to 5 PM

If you have children along, this is a good day to indulge them with a visit to this hands-on museum with more than 250 exhibits, educational programs, a gift shop, an outdoor science park and a seasonal 18-hole miniature golf course. (Admission: Adults, $8; Seniors, $7; Children from ages 3 to 17, $6). Purchase a passport for the Carl Sagan Memorial Planet Walk, series of 11 interactive stone monoliths, each one representing an item in the solar system, distanced throughout the city over the span of three quarters of a mile to an exact 1:5 billion scale of said solar system. The installation was created in memory of Cornell Professor Carl Sagan, a founding member of the museum's advisory board.

>*Get back onto Route 13 heading south and make a right turn onto State Street, then left onto Brindley Street, across the single-lane bridge to Taber Street.*

PORTS OF NEW YORK

815 Taber Street, Ithaca, NY 14850
Phone: (607) 220-6317
Online: www.portsofnewyork.com

It's not only the region's most eccentric winery, it's a treasure trove of history. Frédéric Bouché contracts for premium local grapes to make fortified, Port-inspired wines at an enterprise that doubles as a museum of sorts. Frédéric is on hand to pour tastings of his handcrafted wines and tell stories about the vintage winemaking tools he inherited from La Maison Bouché, the winery his family established in Normandy in 1919.

>*Continue on Taber Street, turn left onto Cecil Malone Drive, then right onto Route 13 heading south to Newfield (about 15 minutes).*

1853 COVERED BRIDGE

In the Town of Newfield, a few miles south of Ithaca and a short drive off Route 13, stands the oldest surviving covered bridge still open to daily vehicular traffic, built by Samuel Hamm and Sons and dedicated to Elijah Moore, the son of an early settler. It crosses the west branch of the Cayuga Creek in a single span of 115 feet. The bridge underwent a complete repair in 1972 when a laminated arch was added to the original truss.

>*Get back onto Route 13 heading north to Ithaca.*

BUTTERMILK FALLS

Just before entering the city of Ithaca, turn right onto Buttermilk Falls Road. The main falls, with churning water that looks like buttermilk, is 165 feet high, tumbling in a wide, frothy cascade. It was once a sacred site for the Sapony and Tutelo tribes who lived in the nearby village known as Coreorgonel until it was destroyed in 1779 by General John Sullivan's army in retaliation for British-led Indian raids against the American rebels during the Revolutionary War.

>Get back onto Route 13 heading north to Ithaca, then turn right onto Buffalo Street heading into downtown.

MOOSEWOOD RESTAURANT 🍴

215 North Cayuga Street (at the corner of Seneca Street), Ithaca, NY 14850
Phone: (607) 273-9610
Online: www.moosewoodrestaurant.com
Hours: Sunday-Thursday, 5:30 PM to 8:30 PM, Friday & Saturday, 6 PM to 9 PM
Corkage Fee: $10

Back in the era of Richard Nixon and Earth Shoes, seven friends opened Moosewood Restaurant in the basement of the old Ithaca High School building, unaware that they were making culinary history. Mothership of the legendary vegetarian cookbook, *Bon Appetit* listed Moosewood among the most influential American restaurants of the past century. Anchored in what is now the Dewitt Mall, the restaurant is Ithaca's hometown vegetarian mainstay, where for over forty years they have been serving hearty, meat-free, comfort food minus the sanctimony.

>Take Seneca Street heading west across, the turn right onto Route 13 North.

PURITY ICE CREAM 🍴

Route 13 North at Cascadilla Street, Ithaca, NY 14850
Phone: (607) 272-1545
Online: www.purityicecream.com

Following church services on a Sunday in the spring of 1892, Reverend John M. Scott visited the Platt & Colt Pharmacy in downtown Ithaca for his usual dish of vanilla ice cream. That day, instead of plain vanilla for the Reverend, Chester Platt dipped his scoop of ice cream into a champagne coupe, poured cherry syrup over the top, and dressed it with a candied cherry. Scott proposed that it be named after the day on which it was invented: Cherry Sunday! Since Ithaca is widely accepted as the birthplace of the ice cream sundae, there's no better place for dessert than Purity Ice Cream, a local pleasure palace that has been crafting freshly-made ice creams into sundaes since 1936.

>*Follow Route 13 South, then turn left onto Buffalo Street heading east across downtown.*

WILLIAM HENRY MILLER INN 🛏

303 North Aurora Street, Ithaca, NY 14850
Phone: (607) 256-4553
Online: www.millerinn.com

William Henry Miller, an 1872 graduate of the architecture school at Cornell, became the foremost architect in Ithaca, designing over seventy buildings on and off the university campus, including this downtown home commissioned by the Stowell family. Travel back in time and stay overnight in a meticulously-managed B&B with a choice of nine guest rooms, all with private baths, two with 2-person Jacuzzis, and one with whirlpool/shower combination tub. A lovely dessert buffet is offered before bedtime, and homemade breads and jams accompany splendid breakfast fare.

Entry Point:

ITHACA

(SOUTH - EAST)

SCENIC & HISTORIC

WEEKEND TOUR

Friday

TAVERNA BANFI

130 Statler Drive, Ithaca, NY 14853
Phone: (607) 254-2565
Online: www.tavernabanfi.com
Dinner Hours: 6 PM to 11 PM
Corkage Fee: $25.

Situated on the second floor of the Statler Hotel at Cornell University, the restaurant offers a Tuscan-theme menu and the ambiance of an Italian trattoria. Search for the small handful of local bottles in a wine list packed with selections from Cornell alumni-owned Banfi Vintners.

THE STATLER HOTEL

130 Statler Drive (Cornell University Campus), Ithaca, NY 14853
Phone: (800) 541-2501
Online: www.statlerhotel.cornell.edu

The hotel is operated by the venerable School of Hotel Administration at Cornell, so expect impeccable accommodations and service from the front desk employees to the valet attendants and restaurant staff. Cocktails and small-plate menu available in the Regent Lounge.

Saturday

TAVERNA BANFI

130 Statler Drive, Ithaca, NY 14853
Phone: (607) 254-2565
Online: www.tavernabanfi.com
Hours: 7 AM to 11 AM

Situated on the second floor of the Statler Hotel at Cornell University, the restaurant offers a tasteful breakfast, from the buffet or a la carte.

CORNELL UNIVERSITY 👀

Consistently ranked among the top 20 universities in the world, Cornell sits on a hilltop overlooking 40-mile-long Cayuga Lake and teems with intellectual energy. Two sides of the campus are bound by gorges, cut during the last 12,000 years. Creeks and waterfalls fill the gorges, and no matter where you are on campus you are never far from the sight and sound of falling water. A quiet Saturday morning is a good time to visit. Pick up the morning paper at Willard Straight Hall and stroll along the historic Arts Quad where you'll hear the ring of chimes from McGraw Tower played by student chimemasters every 15 minutes a day during the school year, with a reduced number of performances when classes are not in session.

HERBERT F. JOHNSON MUSEUM OF ART 👀

114 Central Avenue, Ithaca, NY 14853
Phone: (607) 255-6464
Hours: 10 AM to 5 PM
Online: www.museum.cornell.edu

This is your day for serious art appreciation. Built on the crest of Cornell's Library Slope, the very spot where Ezra Cornell determined the location for his university, the Johnson Museum, designed by architect I.M. Pei, houses more than 35,000 works of art in its permanent collection, including works by William Hogarth, Francisco Goya, Édouard Manet, Charles-François Daubigny, Edgar Degas, Henri de Toulouse-Lautrec, and Henri Matisse. There are also extensive holdings of American artists, including Georgia O'Keeffe and Andy Warhol. The main pedestrian access is from the Arts Quad to the east.

SUSPENSION BRIDGE 👀

Designed by two Cornell professors and built in 1960, the pedestrian bridge crosses 138 feet above Fall Creek, connecting students who live on North Campus to Central Campus. According to Cornell legend, if a couple crosses the suspension bridge and the young woman does not accept a kiss from her partner, the bridge will collapse into the gorge. If the kiss is accepted, the couple is assured a long future together.

>*From University Avenue, turn left onto Stewart Avenue, then right onto Buffalo Street heading into downtown. Make a left turn onto Cayuga Street.*

MOOSEWOOD RESTAURANT 🍴

215 North Cayuga Street (at the corner of Seneca Street), Ithaca, NY 14850
Phone: (607) 273-9610
Online: www.moosewoodrestaurant.com
Lunch Hours: 11:30 AM to 3 PM
Corkage Fee: $10

Like *The Simpsons* and Tony Bennett, certain restaurants have weathered the test of time. Mothership of the legendary vegetarian cookbook, *Bon Appetit* listed Moosewood among the most influential restaurants of the past century. Anchored in a school-building-turned-alternative-mall, the restaurant is Ithaca's hometown vegetarian mainstay, where for over forty years they have been serving imaginative, meat-free, comfort food minus the sanctimony. The worker-owned business model is part of the uniqueness of Moosewood, the source of its sustained energy and culinary creativity.

THE HISTORY CENTER 🔭

401 East State/MLK Jr. Street, Ithaca, NY 14850
Phone: (607) 273-8284
Hours: 11 AM to 5 PM
Online: www.thehistorycenter.net

Wend your way back to Ithaca for a visit to the History Center and get to know what makes the city tick. Explore Ithaca and Tompkins County through beautifully curated museum exhibits and a research library for casual readers and scholars, school children, local historians, genealogists, and professional researchers.

>*Take Seneca Street heading west across downtown, then turn right onto Route 89 (Taughannock Boulevard) heading north along the west shore of Cayuga Lake.*

TAUGHANNOCK FALLS 🔭

Take a short drive off Route 89 onto Taughannock Park Road to gawk at New York State's highest waterfall, dropping 215 feet past rocky cliffs that tower nearly 400 feet above the gorge, making it 33 feet taller than Niagara Falls and one of the largest single-drop waterfalls east of the Rocky Mountains. Legend has it that the falls are named for a Lenape (Delaware) Indian chief named Taughannock who, upon leading his tribe to invade the local Cayuga people, was thrown from the top of his cliff to his demise in the pools below. Gorge and rim trails provide spectacular views of the "hanging valley" from above and below. Visitors in autumn can enjoy the picturesque colors of the surrounding trees. The adjacent park offers hiking and nature trails, camping, picnicking, swimming, fishing, and a boat launch.

BELLWETHER CIDERY 🍷

9070 Route 89, Trumansburg, NY 14886
Phone: (607) 387-9464
Online: www.cidery.com

The wide choice of locally-grown apples gives Bellwether cidermaker Bill Barton a lot to work with, and the results are exceptional varietals and blends. Many of his ciders are concocted from varieties usually considered "eating apples." Empire, Gala, and Fuji are combined in the semi-dry "Original" Hard Cider. "Liberty Spy" has a hearty taste and succulent mouthfeel from the blend of Liberty and Northern Spy apples; the marriage of local Tompkins King and Baldwin produces a tart, refreshing quaff called "King Baldwin." Bellwether's Heritage Hard Cider includes up to 25 varieties of bittersweets and bittersharps (with names like Somerset Redstreak, Tremlett's Bitter, Harry Masters Jersey, and Brown Snout) for a full-bodied drink of rich complexity in a food-friendly style that could rival a fine Riesling.

CAYUGA RIDGE ESTATE WINERY 🍷

6800 Route 89, Ovid, NY 14521
Phone: (607) 869-5158
Online: www.cayugaridgewinery.com

Most hybrid grapes were developed by French scientists between 1880 and 1950. Their goal was to combine the finer taste characteristics of European vinifera varieties with the winter-hardiness and disease-resistance of the Native-American varieties. Hybrid varieties continue to be developed specifically for the Finger Lakes and other cool climate regions by the Cornell University's New York State Agricultural Experiment Station. The grand old cavernous barn at Cayuga Ridge provides a rustic setting for tasting a good to terrific range of wines, in particular, Cayuga White, a regional hybrid cross, developed at the Experiment Station in 1972. The mother-block of Cayuga White at Cayuga Ridge, blanketing 8 acres of the vineyard with vigorous clusters of greenish-gold, translucent grapes is entrusted to Tom Challen, a skilled grower and winemaker from Canadian wine country. It's an easy-to-enjoy "sipping wine," often compared to Pinot Grigio. Wood-fired pizzas offered here on summer weekends, Fridays, Saturdays and Sundays from 11:30 AM to 5:30 PM.

>*Continue on Route 89 heading north. Just past the New York Chiropractic College, make a left onto Route 116 and continue to Seneca Falls (about 30 minutes).*

GOULD HOTEL

108 Fall Street (Routes 5&20), Seneca Falls, NY 13148
Phone: (877) 788-4010
Online: www.thegouldhotel.com
Corkage Fee: $15
Dinner Hours: 5 PM to 10 PM

The first all-metal pump in the world was cast and assembled in a little stone shop at Green and Ovid Streets in Seneca Falls by Seabury S. Gould's manufacturing company. Goulds Pumps became the world's largest company dedicated to producing only pumps (acquired by ITT Technology in 1997). Construction of the red brick, four-story hotel on Fall Street began in 1919, named The Gould Hotel after its main financier, Norman J. Gould, grandson of the company's founder. The grand old Gould has been revitalized with well-appointed 48 guest rooms and restaurant. The handsome dining room of the Gould offers charcuterie and cheese plates, sandwiches, stone oven pizzas, and a wide range of main plates.

PENNY'S PLACE

2109 Routes 5&20, Seneca Falls, NY 13148
Phone: (315) 568-8746
Breakfast Hours: 5 AM to 1 PM

Walk into this family restaurant, ensconced in the Liberty Plaza strip mall, and it's hard not to feel right at home. Celebrate the simple pleasure of maple syrup atop a stack of pancakes or other well-prepared breakfast fare with homespun style among a cavalcade of characterful customers.

SENECA FALLS

The village is named for the series of small falls and rapids on the Seneca River which drains both Cayuga and Seneca Lakes. Residents claim that when director Frank Capra visited Seneca Falls in 1945, he was inspired to model fictional Bedford Falls in the holiday film classic *It's a Wonderful Life* after their town. Local businessman Norman J. Gould, one of the richest men in town, had great control over politics and economics of the area, much as Henry F. Potter did in the movie. Take a walk across the steel truss bridge over the Cayuga-Seneca Canal, a close match to the bridge that George Bailey jumped from to save Clarence the angel.

NATIONAL WOMEN'S HALL OF FAME

76 Fall Street (Routes 5&20), Seneca Falls, NY 13148
Phone: (315) 568-8060
Online: www.greatwomen.org
Hours: 12 Noon to 5 PM (May thru September)

Dedicated to recognizing and celebrating the achievements of great American women to the arts, athletics, business, education, government, the humanities, philanthropy and science, the Women's Hall of Fame is a worthy stop on a visit to Seneca Falls. Adult admission to the gallery exhibit is $3 (Students/Seniors $1.50).

SENECA MUSEUM OF WATERWAYS AND INDUSTRY

89 Fall Street (Routes 5&20), Seneca Falls, NY 13148
Phone: (315) 568-1510
Online: www.senecamuseum.com
Hours: 12 Noon to 4 PM

The Cayuga-Seneca Canal was connected to the Erie Canal by 1828 and is presently part of the Erie Barge Canal system. The Museum illustrates how the Seneca River and the Cayuga-Seneca Canal powered the rise of industry and fostered cultural development, helping to spread social reform movements. Free admission.

>Follow Routes 5&20 heading east, just past the intersection of Route 89.

MONTEZUMA WINERY

2981 Routes 5&20, Seneca Falls, NY 13148
Phone: (315) 568-8190
Online: www.montezumawinery.com

The Martin family translates the fragrant essence of apples, strawberries, blueberries, raspberries, cranberries, peaches, plums, and rhubarb from local farms and orchards into stand-alone fruit wines that provide a taste of fruit at the peak of the season. A sister operation, Hidden Marsh Distillery, produces liqueurs, vodka, and brandy made with honey, apples, and other seasonal fruits.

>Continue on Routes 5&20 heading east to Route 90 heading south.

MACKENZIE-CHILDS 🛒

3260 Route 90, Aurora, NY 13026
Phone: (888) 665-1999
Online: www.mackenzie-childs.com
Hours: Daily, 9:30 AM to 6:30 PM

A winding red brick road leads to a working production studio where whimsical, handmade ceramics, enamelware, glassware, furniture, and home furnishings. Tour the manufacturing process to observe artisans hand-forming, hand-painting, and hand-trimming each extraordinary piece.

AURORA INN

391 Main Street (Route 90), Aurora , NY 13026
Phone: (315) 364-8888
Online: www.aurora-inn.com
Hours: Call for schedule
Corkage Fee: $15.

By the mid-19th century, Aurora was a major stop on the Erie Canal for boats carrying agricultural products from area farmers to New York City. In 1833, Colonel E. B. Morgan, a native of Aurora and original investor in *The New York Times,* built the Aurora Inn, now listed on the National Register of Historic Places. In summer, lunch on the lakeside patio is an idyllic scene right off the pages of a Jane Austen novel. The kitchen takes a bold approach to flavors with an artist's notion of presentation. The wine list includes a thoughtful mix of local red and white varieties that are likely to match up with the food.

BET THE FARM WINERY AND GOURMET MARKET

381 Main Street (Route 90), Aurora, NY 13026
Phone: (315) 294-5643
Online: www.betthefarmny.com

While you're in the neighborhood, do as the neighbors do and stop into Bet the Farm. The combination winery tasting room and market operated by Nancy Tisch is the darling of the village of Aurora. Nancy's handmade wines share shelf space with bottles from neighboring wineries, as well as an assortment of flatbreads, dressings, dipping sauces, jams, maple syrups, biscotti, and chocolates from small-scale producers.

WELLS COLLEGE

Established as a woman's college in 1868 by Henry Wells, founder of Wells Fargo and the American Express Company, Wells became a co-educational institution in 2005. The campus is situated on 365 beautifully landscaped acres in the small, picturesque village of Aurora, nestled on the shore of Cayuga Lake. According to tradition, the college president declares a school holiday when Cayuga Lake freezes over. In 1875, student Emma Lampert skated across the lake and back, and numerous excursions in horse-drawn sleds were reported. The tradition has been maintained in years 1912, 1918, 1934, 1948, 1962, and 1979.

>*Continue on Route 90 heading south to King Ferry. Make a right turn onto Route 34B (Ridge Road), then a right turn onto Center Road. Continue to the intersection of Lake Road.*

KING FERRY WINERY (TRELEAVEN WINES)

658 Lake Road, King Ferry, NY 13081
Phone: (315) 364-5100
Online: www.treleavenwines.com

He was known on Capitol Hill as "the gentlemanly gentleman from Massachusetts." After serving three terms as governor and four terms in the U.S. Senate, Leverett Saltonstall stepped down from public service to become a gentleman farmer. His oldest son, also named Leverett, eschewed politics and, instead, distinguished himself in agriculture as professor of agronomy at Cornell, cattle rancher, and seed producer on the 700-acre Treleaven Farm, bordering the eastern shore of Cayuga Lake. On a pasture where beef cattle once roamed, wine grapes now flourish. While the winery surely made its name with big, oak-y Chardonnays, in the last several years Peter and Taci Saltonstall have produced extraordinary, terroir-driven Rieslings, consistently showing well in competitions.

>*Follow Lake Road heading south to Ridge Road (Route 34B). Turn right onto Route 34 heading south to Ithaca (about 10 minutes). Take Route 13 heading south and drive to Newfield (about 15 minutes). Follow signs to the covered bridge.*

1853 COVERED BRIDGE

In the Town of Newfield, a few miles south of Ithaca and a short drive off Route 13, stands the oldest surviving covered bridge still open to daily vehicular traffic, built by Samuel Hamm and Sons and dedicated to Elijah Moore, the son of an early settler. It crosses the west branch of the Cayuga Creek in a single span of 115 feet. The bridge underwent a complete repair in 1972 when a laminated arch was added to the original truss.

>*Get back onto Route 13 heading north to Ithaca.*

BUTTERMILK FALLS 🔭

Just before entering the city of Ithaca, turn right onto Buttermilk Falls Road. The main falls, with churning water that looks like buttermilk, is 165 feet high, tumbling in a wide, frothy cascade. A natural pool at the base of the falls provides a popular local swimming hole. Upstream, a scenic trail circles Lake Treman. This was once a sacred site for the Sapony and Tutelo tribes who lived in the nearby village known as Coreorgonel until it was destroyed during the Revolutionary War by the Sullivan Expedition of 1779. George Washington had ordered retaliation for British-led Indian raids against the American rebels.

>*Get back onto Route 13 heading north to Ithaca. Make a right onto Willow Avenue, an immediate left onto Lincoln Street, then turn left onto Tioga Street.*

NORTHSTAR HOUSE 🍴

202 East Falls Street, Ithaca, NY 14850
Phone: (607) 216-8580
Online: www.northstarpub.com
Corkage Fee: $15

We should all be so lucky to have a spot like Northstar as our neighborhood gathering place. It's a young, punchy enterprise that seems to strike just the right notes. A hyperactive tap list and an exhaustive selection of bottled craft beers are enough to convince you it's a legitimate bar, but the deliciously scattershot menu with truly a little something for every mood makes it part-restaurant, too. The organic chicken wings are offered in three versions — with BBQ sauce, mild to hot Buffalo-style sauce, or Baltimore-style, tossed in brown butter and Old Bay seasoning. After dinner, hoof it over to Ithaca Falls, just a block away, and follow the trail to the bottom of the falls for a breathtaking view. At 105 feet high and 175 feet wide, Ithaca Falls is a massive jumble of irregular cascades and overhanging drops.

>*Reverse course and return to Route 13 heading south.*

PURITY ICE CREAM 🍴

Route 13 at Cascadilla Street, Ithaca, NY 14850
Phone: (607) 272-1545
Online: www.purityicecream.com

Following church services on a Sunday in the spring of 1892, Reverend John M. Scott visited the Platt & Colt Pharmacy in downtown Ithaca for his usual dish of vanilla ice cream. That day, instead of plain vanilla for the Reverend, Chester Platt dipped his scoop of ice cream into a champagne coupe, poured cherry syrup over the top, and dressed it with a candied cherry. Scott proposed that it be named after the day on which it was invented: Cherry Sunday! Since Ithaca is widely accepted as the birthplace of the ice cream sundae, there's no better place for dessert than Purity Ice Cream, a local pleasure palace that has been crafting freshly-made ice creams into sundaes since 1936.

>Follow Route 13 South, then turn left onto Buffalo Street heading east across downtown.

WILLIAM HENRY MILLER INN 🛏

303 North Aurora Street, Ithaca, NY 14850
Phone: (607) 256-4553
Online: www.millerinn.com

William Henry Miller, an 1872 graduate of the architecture school at Cornell, became the foremost architect in Ithaca for many years, designing over seventy buildings on and off the university campus, including this downtown home commissioned by the Stowell family. Travel back in time and stay overnight in a meticulously-managed B&B with a choice of nine guest rooms, all with private bath, two with 2-person Jacuzzis, and one with whirlpool/shower combination tub. A lovely dessert buffet is offered before bedtime, and homemade breads and jams accompany splendid breakfast fare.

Entry Point:

SKANEATELES

(NORTH - EAST)

SCENIC & HISTORIC

DAY TRIP

BLUEWATER GRILL 🍴

11 West Genesse Street (Route 20), Skaneateles, NY 13152
Phone: (315) 685-6600
Hours: Open for breakfast at 8 AM

Perched on the north shore of Skaneateles Lake, Bluewater offers a full breakfast menu with all the necessities. Ask for a table on the outside deck overlooking the bluish-green waters of the lake and imbibe some local color.

CLIFT PARK 🔭

Skaneateles is a charming and somewhat eccentric village nestled at the north end of the lake, where antique shops and boutiques flourish in the business district (malls and fast-food outlets are outlawed). The first settlers were veterans of the Revolutionary War who were awarded land grants as compensation for military service. Clift Park (named for Joab Lawrence Clift, local farmer and businessman) in the heart of the village has a gazebo, several park benches, and a long pier that walks out onto the lake, used for fishing by many locals and picture-taking by visitors.

>*Take Route 20 heading west to Auburn, then turn left onto South Street.*

SEWARD HOUSE 🔭

33 South Street, Auburn, NY 13021
Phone: (315) 252-1283
Online: www.sewardhouse.org
Hours: daily (except Monday), 10 AM to 4 PM

William H. Seward served as New York State Governor, U.S. Senator and Secretary of State to Presidents Abraham Lincoln and Andrew Johnson. His Auburn estate, surrounded by two acres of lush garden and trees, has been restored to its original beauty and features a collection of political and travel souvenirs, decorative arts and photographs that spans Seward's nearly forty-year political career. South Street includes a collection of other magnificent old homes, including the Case Mansion (62 South Street), a four-floor Jacobean Revival structure with an indoor swimming pool, great hall and ballroom, built by Theodore Case with the profits earned from the sale of his process for adding sound to movies (now home to the mental health residential program of Unity House).

HARRIET TUBMAN HOME 👀

180 South Street, Auburn NY 13201
Phone: (315) 252-2081
Online: www.harriethouse.org
Hours: 10 AM to 3 PM

During the Civil War, Harriet Tubman, herself an escaped slave, served with the Union Army as a cook, laundress, nurse, scout, and spy behind Confederate lines. Her home, restored in 1953 and furnished with mementoes from Harriet's time here, was her base of operations while aiding fugitives from slavery along the "Underground Railroad" to Free States and Canada. (The brick house to the south was Harriet Tubman's actual home, built by her second husband who was a brick maker).

>Get back onto Routes 5&20 heading west to Waterloo.

MAC'S DRIVE-IN 🍴

1166 Waterloo-Geneva Road (Routes 5&20), Waterloo, NY 13165
Phone: (315) 539-3064
Online: www.macsdrivein.net
Hours: 10:30 AM to 10 PM (Closed Monday)

The heyday of drive-ins may be decades in the past, but drive-in culture still flourishes a half mile west of the village of Waterloo. Since 1961, when the juke box played "Let's Twist Again," the MacDougal family has faithfully maintained car-hop service from a menu which includes hamburgers, French fries, and "chicken-in-a-basket" washed down with root beer and milkshakes. The ice cream window offers sundaes and banana splits. (Eat-in dining available).

>Continue west on Routes 5&20 to Seneca Falls.

SENECA FALLS 👀

The village is named for the series of small falls and rapids on the Seneca River which drain both Cayuga and Seneca Lakes. Residents claim that when director Frank Capra visited Seneca Falls in 1945, he was inspired to model fictional Bedford Falls in the holiday film classic *It's a Wonderful Life* after their town. Local businessman Norman J. Gould, one of the richest men in town, had great control over politics and economics of the area, much as Henry F. Potter did in the movie. Take a walk across the steel truss bridge over the Cayuga-Seneca Canal, a close match to the bridge that George Bailey jumped from to save Clarence the angel.

NATIONAL WOMEN'S HALL OF FAME

76 Fall Street, Seneca Falls, NY 13148
Phone: (315) 568-8060
Online: www.greatwomen.org
Hours: Monday thru Saturday, 10 AM to 5 PM; Sunday 12 Noon to 5 PM

Early women's rights leaders Elizabeth Cady Stanton, Lucretia Coffin Mott, Martha Coffin Wright, Mary Ann McClintock and Jane Hunt hastily organized an influential Women's Rights Convention, also known as the Seneca Falls Convention, held here in 1848. The Hall of Fame is dedicated to recognizing and celebrating the achievements of great American women to the arts, athletics, business, education, government, the humanities, philanthropy and science. Adult admission to the gallery exhibit is $3 (Students/Seniors $1.50).

SENECA MUSEUM OF WATERWAYS AND INDUSTRY

89 Fall Street, Seneca Falls, NY 13148
Phone: (315) 568-1510
Online: www.senecamuseum.com
Hours: Monday thru Saturday, 10 AM to 4 PM; Sunday, 12 Noon to 4 PM

The Cayuga-Seneca Canal was connected to the Erie Canal by 1828 and is presently part of the Erie Barge Canal system. The Museum illustrates how the Seneca River and the Cayuga-Seneca Canal powered the rise of industry and fostered cultural development, helping to spread social reform movements. Free admission.

>*Get back onto Routes 5&20 heading east, returning to Skaneateles.*

SKANEATELES MUSEUM AT THE CREAMERY 👀

28 Hannum Street (off Route 20), Skaneateles, NY 13152
Phone: (315) 685-1360
Online: www.skaneateleshistoricalsociety.org
Hours: Thursday thru Sunday, 1 PM to 4 PM

Originally a place for local farmers to sell their milk and for residents to buy dairy products, the Creamery is now a museum and a home to the local Historical Society. The artifact collection features hundreds of items related to farming, manufacturing, recreation, transportation, art, architecture, the press, and commerce. Of special interest are the locally manufactured boats, carriages, wooden toys, medical instruments, sleigh, and chairs.

THE KREBS 🍴

53 West Genesee Street (Route 20), Skaneateles, NY 13152
Phone: (315) 685-1800
Online: www.thekrebs.com
Corkage Fee: $25
Dinner Hours: 5:30 to 10:30 PM (Thursday, Friday and Saturday only)

Housed in a building that dates to 1845, the restaurant was opened in 1899 by Fred and Cora Krebs, and remained in the family until 2010. At different periods in its history, the restaurant served dinner to Presidents Franklin Delano Roosevelt and William Jefferson Clinton. Re-vamped and re-opened in 2014 by scrap metal magnate Adam Weitsman, the old girl has a fresh, over-the-top interior and an updated version of its famous Lobster Newburg on the menu. In an extraordinary gesture, Weitsman donates all net profits earned by the restaurant to women's and children's charities in Central New York.

SHERWOOD INN 🛏️

26 West Genesee Street (Route 20), Skaneateles, NY 13152
Phone: (315) 685-3405
Online: www.thesherwoodinn.com

When Isaac Sherwood won a contract to carry mail west from Onondaga Hill, he carried it on foot. But soon he was aided by a horse, then a wagon, and finally a stagecoach. From the stagecoach, he built an empire, owning and investing in stage lines running across New York from Albany to Buffalo. Isaac Sherwood's name lives on at the Sherwood Inn, built on the site of the inn he first raised to serve weary stagecoach passengers 1807. (During the historic "Knickerbocker Tour" of 1822, visitors from New York City stopped at the Sherwood on their way to Niagara Falls). After dinner, take a stroll to Clift Park across the street, then repair to one of the 15 comfortable, antique-appointed guest rooms, each with private bath and each restored and decorated to retain the setting's period charm.

Entry Point:

SKANEATELES

(NORTH - EAST)

SCENIC & HISTORIC

WEEKEND TOUR

Friday

ROSALIE'S CUCINA 🍴

841 West Genesee Street (Route 20), Skaneateles, NY 13152
Phone: (315) 685-2200
Online: www.rosaliescucina.com
Hours: 5 PM to 10 PM
Corkage Fee: $20 (limit 2 bottles per table)

This remarkable restaurant is the brainstorm of Auburn native Phil Romano, who earned a national reputation with multi-unit theme eateries including Romano's Macaroni Grill. Rosalie's has the same engaging Italian fare, only it's slightly more upscale and a bit pricier. It's difficult to say what's best about Rosalie's — the bustling, high-energy setting, the well-trained servers, or the terrific food. And for enthusiasts wanting to match local wine to the restaurant's Tuscan cuisine, Rosalie's offers a handful of well-chosen bottles.

FINGER LAKES LODGING 🛏

834 West Genesee Street (Route 20), Skaneateles, NY 13152
Phone: (315) 217-0222
Online: www.fingerlakeslodging.com

Not as luxurious as Mirbeau, its sister property across the street (and next to Rosalie's), this former motel has been upgraded with Adirondack flourishes and clean, comfortable rooms. Best bet for an overnight stay, plus you can enjoy the spa amenities at Mirabeau for a small fee without the price of staying there.

Saturday

BLUEWATER GRILL 🍴

11 West Genesse Street (Route 20), Skaneateles, NY 13152
Phone: (315) 685-6600
Hours: Open for breakfast at 8 AM

Perched on the north shore of Skaneateles Lake, Bluewater offers a full breakfast menu with all the necessities. Ask for a table on the outside deck overlooking the bluish-green waters of the lake and imbibe some local color.

CLIFT PARK 👀

Skaneateles is a charming and somewhat eccentric village nestled at the north end of the lake, where antique shops and boutiques flourish in the business district (malls and fast-food outlets are outlawed). The first settlers were veterans of the Revolutionary War who were awarded land grants as compensation for military service. Clift Park (named for Joab Lawrence Clift, local farmer and businessman) in the heart of the village has a gazebo, several park benches, and a long pier that walks out onto the lake, used for fishing by many locals and picture-taking by visitors.

>*Take Route 20 heading west to Auburn, then turn left onto South Street.*

SEWARD HOUSE 👀

33 South Street, Auburn, NY 13021
Phone: (315)252-1283
Online: www.sewardhouse.org
Hours: 10 AM to 4 PM

William H. Seward served as New York State Governor, U.S. Senator and Secretary of State to Presidents Abraham Lincoln and Andrew Johnson. His Auburn estate, surrounded by two acres of lush garden and trees, has been restored to its original beauty and features a collection of political and travel souvenirs, decorative arts and photographs that spans Seward's nearly forty-year political career. Another magnificent old home on South Street, the Case Mansion (62 South Street), a four-floor Jacobean Revival structure with an indoor swimming pool, great hall and ballroom, was built by Theodore Willard Case with the profits earned from the sale of his process for adding optical sound to movies (now home to the mental health residential program of Unity House).

HARRIET TUBMAN HOME

180 South Street, Auburn NY 13201
Phone: (315) 252-2081
Online: www.harriethouse.org
Hours: 10 AM to 3 PM

During the Civil War, Harriet Tubman, herself an escaped slave, served with the Union Army as a cook, laundress, nurse, scout, and spy behind Confederate lines. Her home, restored in 1953 and furnished with mementoes from Harriet's time here, was her base of operations while aiding fugitives from slavery along the "Underground Railroad" to Free States and Canada. (The brick house to the south was Harriet Tubman's actual home, built by her second husband who was a brick maker).

>Drive back across Routes 5&20 as South Street becomes North Street. Turn right on Seminary Street, then left onto Nelson Street.

WILLARD MEMORIAL CHAPEL

17 Nelson Street, Auburn NY 13021
Phone: 315-252-0339
Online: www.willardchapel.org
Hours: Call for info

From 1892 to 1894, the Willard Chapel was built and furnished in memory of Dr. Sylvester Willard and his wife, Mrs. Jane Frances Case Willard, by their daughters Miss Georgiana and Miss Caroline Willard. It is the only surviving chapel boasting of a complete and unaltered interior designed by Louis Comfort Tiffany, the American artist most associated with Art Nouveau, including his works in stained glass windows, leaded glass chandeliers, mosaic floors, and gold-stenciled furniture, ceiling and pulpit. ($3 admission)

>Drive back to Routes 5&20 heading west, then turn right onto State Street.

AUBURN CORRECTIONAL FACILITY

135 State Street, Auburn, NY 13024

There are no public tours, but it's just a short diversion to view this state maximum security facility, built on land that was once a Cayuga Indian village. It was the first prison to implement the "Auburn System," a penal method that promised to rehabilitate criminals by teaching them personal discipline and respect for work, property, and other people. Inmates have ranged from Leon Czolgosz, the assassin of President William McKinley, who was electrocuted in Auburn on October 29, 1901, to Robert Chambers, the "preppy murderer," who served his full 15 year sentence here. The statue of a colonial soldier atop the apex is called "Copper John."

>*Drive back to Routes 5&20 heading west to Waterloo (about 25 minutes).*

MAC'S DRIVE-IN 🍴

1166 Waterloo-Geneva Road (Routes 5&20), Waterloo, NY 13165
Phone: (315) 539-3064
Online: www.macsdrivein.net
Hours: 10:30 AM to 10 PM

The heyday of drive-ins may be decades in the past, but drive-in culture still flourishes a half mile west of the village of Waterloo. Since 1961, when the juke box played "Let's Twist Again," the MacDougal family has faithfully maintained car-hop service from a menu which includes hamburgers, French fries, and "chicken-in-a-basket" washed down with root beer and milkshakes. The ice cream window offers sundaes and banana splits. (Eat-in dining available).

>*Continue on Routes 5&20 heading west to Geneva.*

GENEVA SOUTH MAIN STREET 🔭

Online: www.southmainst.com

A walking tour starts at 380 South Main Street, the corner of William Street and South Main. The South Main Street Historic District extends from Seneca Street south to Conover Street, including 140 structures as well as Pulteney Park and the original quad of the Hobart College campus.

>*Take Routes 5&20 to Route 96A heading south.*

VENTOSA VINEYARDS

3440 Route 96A (just south of Routes 5&20), Geneva, NY 14456
Phone: (315) 719-0000
Online: www.ventosavineyards.com

His grandparents grew grapes in the wine region of southern Italy. Lenny Cecere made a fortune building theme parks and commercial swim and water parks around the world. Retired in 1997, he purchased a 107-year-old Geneva farmhouse on 65 acres that was in foreclosure, turning the land into vineyards, winemaking facility, and tasting room. Ventosa (Italian for "windy") offers several Old World-influenced wines fashioned from well-tended vines. This is the place to taste Sangiovese, a rare varietal in the region, as well as the region's only plantings of Tocai Friulano, a Northern Italian classic called "the wine that makes friends easily."

>Reverse course on Route 96A heading north.

ROSE HILL MANSION

3373 Route 96A, Geneva, NY 14456
Phone: (315) 789-3848
Online: www.rosehillmansion.com
Hours: 10 AM to 4 PM

One of the finest examples of the Greek Revival Style in the United States, Rose Hill was built in 1837 on a military tract granted to Revolutionary War soldiers. Its monumental scale reflects the prosperity of Western New York as a result of the Erie Canal. The property was declared a National Historic Landmark in 1986.

>Drive back to Routes 5&20, then take Route 14 heading south.

GENEVA ON THE LAKE

1001 Lochland Road (Route 14), Geneva, NY 14456
Phone: (315) 789-7190
Online: www.genevaonthelake.com
Corkage Fee: $17

One of the genuine treats of the Finger Lakes. Built in 1914 as a private home and modeled after the Lancelotti villa in the hills of Frascati near

Rome, its interior includes Italian marble fireplaces, tapestries, Ionic columns and wood-coffered ceilings. The villa later became a monastery, and then, in 1981, a boutique hotel, managed with impeccable expertise by Bill Schickel. The Lancellotti Dining Room provides a courtly setting for candlelight dinner (local wine-pairing flight available). Flaming desserts served tableside. The mood brightens in summer when the doors are thrown open for patio dining. After a stroll amid spectacular lakeside gardens and classical sculptures, settle in to one of the suites or studios appointed with Stickley furniture. The period atmosphere evokes a gentler time, and it is very easy to get lost in the moment here.

Sunday

GENEVA ON THE LAKE 🍴

1001 Lochland Road (Route 14), Geneva, NY 14456
Phone: (315) 789-7190
Online: www.genevaonthelake.com

Watch the sunrise over Seneca Lake, then have "al fresco" breakfast on The Terrace, overlooking the spectacular lakeside gardens.

>*Take Route 14 heading north to Routes 5&20. Drive east to Waterloo.*

NATIONAL MEMORIAL DAY MUSEUM 🔭

35 East Main Street (Routes 5&20), Waterloo, NY 13165
Phone: (315) 539-9611
Online: www.waterloony.com/MdayMus.html
Hours: Call for info

In May of 1966, Waterloo was recognized as the "Birthplace of Memorial Day" by the United States Government. Visitors to the local museum learn the story of the origins of Memorial Day, born out of the unimaginable death toll of the Civil War.

>*Continue on Routes 5&20 heading east to Seneca Falls.*

SENECA FALLS

The village is named for the series of small falls and rapids on the Seneca River which drains both Cayuga and Seneca Lakes. Residents claim that when director Frank Capra visited Seneca Falls in 1945, he was inspired to model fictional Bedford Falls in the holiday film classic *It's a Wonderful Life* after their town. Local businessman Norman J. Gould, one of the richest men in town, had great control over politics and economics of the area, much as Henry F. Potter did in the movie. Take a walk across the steel truss bridge over the Cayuga-Seneca Canal, a close match to the bridge that George Bailey jumped from to save Clarence the angel.

NATIONAL WOMEN'S HALL OF FAME

76 Fall Street, Seneca Falls, NY 13148
Phone: (315) 568-8060
Online: www.greatwomen.org
Hours: 12 Noon to 5 PM

Early women's rights leaders Elizabeth Cady Stanton, Lucretia Coffin Mott, Martha Coffin Wright, Mary Ann McClintock and Jane Hunt hastily organized the influential Seneca Falls Convention, held here in 1848. The Hall of Fame is dedicated to recognizing and celebrating the achievements of great American women to the arts, athletics, business, education, government, the humanities, philanthropy and science. Adult admission to the gallery exhibit is $3 (Students/Seniors $1.50).

ABIGAIL'S RESTAURANT

1978 Routes 5&20, Waterloo, NY 13165
Phone: (315) 539-9300
Online: www.abigailsrestaurant.com
Sunday Hours: Open at 1 PM

The address is Waterloo, but watch for Abigail's just outside of Seneca Falls, a local fixture for over thirty years. Documentary filmmaker Matt Reynolds and a team of judges spent 16 days traveling 2,627 miles and trying 270 types of chicken wings from 72 bars and restaurants along the "Wing Belt" of upstate New York, Pennsylvania, Vermont, and Ontario. By the end of their quest, the "Blue Bayou" wings created by chef Columbus Marshall Grady at Abigail's were named the world's best wings.

SENECA MUSEUM OF WATERWAYS AND INDUSTRY

89 Fall Street, Seneca Falls, NY 13148
Phone: (315) 568-1510
Online: www.senecamuseum.com
Hours: 12 Noon to 4 PM

The Cayuga-Seneca Canal was connected to the Erie Canal by 1828 and is presently part of the Erie Barge Canal system. The Museum illustrates how the Seneca River and the Cayuga-Seneca Canal powered the rise of industry and fostered cultural development, helping to spread social reform movements. Free admission.

>Continue on Routes 5&20 heading east to Skaneateles (about 30 minutes), then turn left onto West Lake Road just before the village.

ANYELA'S VINEYARDS

2433 West Lake Road, Skaneateles, NY 13152
Phone: (315) 685-3797
Online: www.anyelasvineyards.com

Wine devotees will appreciate a side trip, just 5 minutes south of the village. The impressive tasting room reflects the moneyed reputation of Skaneateles and provides a comfortable setting to taste an ambitious range of wines. The style of the Rieslings is one of restraint, not as flamboyantly fruit-driven as some counterparts in the region. The portfolio's strength is with proprietary blends, in which the winemaker adjusts proportions of contributing varietals to the advantages of each year's harvest, i.e. "Overlay," a blend of Cabernet Franc, Pinot Noir, Shiraz and Cabernet Sauvignon.

>Head back to Route 20. Make a right turn into the village.

SKANEATELES MUSEUM AT THE CREAMERY

28 Hannum Street, Skaneateles, NY 13152
Phone: (315) 685-1360
Online: www.skaneateleshistoricalsociety.org
Hours: 1 PM to 4 PM

Originally a place for local farmers to sell their milk and for residents to buy dairy products, the Creamery is now a museum, gift shop, and home to the local Historical Society. The artifact collection features hundreds of items related to farming, manufacturing, recreation, transportation, art, architecture, the press, and commerce. Of special interest are the locally manufactured boats, carriages, wooden toys, medical instruments, sleigh, and chairs.

MIRBEAU INN AND SPA

851 West Genesee Street (Route 20), Skaneateles, NY 13152
Phone: (315) 685-5006
Online: www.mirbeau.com

Stroll the grounds of this luxury hotel/resort complex, set around a water garden and "Japanese bridge" inspired by impressionist painter Claude Monet's magnificent estate at Giverny, then head over to the Wine Bar for a pre-dinner sampling of small pours from nifty, self-serve, dispensing stations. A menu of small plates is offered for sharing and matching up with the wines.

SHERWOOD INN

26 West Genesee Street (Route 20), Skaneateles, NY 13152
Phone: (315) 685-3405
Online: www.thesherwoodinn.com
Corkage Fee: $20

Known as the "Stage Coach King," Isaac Sherwood founded stage lines from Albany to Buffalo which led to the rapid growth of industry and commerce in the Finger Lakes region, and the inn he built for weary stagecoach travelers in 1807 has provided local hospitality ever since. Set in the heart of the village overlooking the lake. Ask for a table in The Tavern for more informal dining (with wood-burning fireplace in the winter months) or on the Lakeview Porch, and feast on America classics such as Yankee Pot Roast and Herb-Roasted Chicken along with a bottle of local wine. After dinner, cross the street to Clift Park, stroll along the shore of what William Henry Seward once described as "the most beautiful body of water in the world," then repair to one of the 15 comfortable, antique-appointed guest rooms, each carefully restored and decorated to retain the setting's period charm..

TASTING GLOSSARY

It's helpful to carry a small notepad with you to tastings so you can jot down your impressions of wines and beers. By evaluating important aspects in each tasting, you refine your palate, pick out subtle details, and better understand the products. The following terms can help you to hone your appreciation, focus on details, and to remember one wine or beer from the next.

Wine Descriptors

Fruits
apple
apricot
banana
blackberry
bramble berries
cherry
coconut
cola
currant
dates
fig
fruit salad
grapefruit
lemon
lime
muskmelon
nectar
orange
olive
papaya
peach
pear
pineapple
plum
pomegranate
prune
raisin
raspberry

strawberry
watermelon

Nuts
almonds
hazelnut
lichee
pecan
walnut

Flavorings
allspice
anise
basil
beer
black pepper
butterscotch
caramel
caraway
cardamom
chocolate
cinnamon
clove
coriander
curry
dill
garlic
ginger
grenadine

honey
juniper
licorice
marjoram
mint
mustard
nutmeg
oregano
paprika
rye
saffron
sage
sesame
soy
turmeric
vanilla

Misc. Food
beef
bell pepper
bread
broccoli
butter
cabbage
celery
cheddar
coffee
cucumber
dough

fish
ham
honey
kraut
lamb
lettuce
malt
mushrooms
oil
onion
parmesan
parsley
pickles
pimento
pork
rancid
rotten egg
sausage
tea
toast
tomato

Other
alum
ammonia
camphor
cardboard
cedar
damp earth
dead leaves
eucalyptus
glue
grass
hay
leather
matches
metallic
mildew
mold
musk

oak
pertoleum
pine
plastic
redwood
resin
rubber
sandalwood
soap
smoke
sweat
talk
tobacco
wet dog

Flowers
apple blossom
carnation
geranium
jasmine
lilac
rose
violet

Balance
balanced
brittle
clumsy
delicate
fat
flabby
graceful
harmonious
imbalanced
inharmonious
lacy
married
puckery
severe
smooth

supple
taut

Style
aristocratic
arresting
charming
character
classic
compelling
distinguished
dull
fancy
flashy
gulpable
languid
lithe
nervous
peacock's tail
presumptuous
refreshing
savoring
seductive
sensitive
sensuous
sipping
sophisticated
stylish
suave
vivacious
winsome

Evaluative
average
flawless
ordinary
palatable
bad
lackluster
objectionable

poor
appealing
attractive
ethereal
excellent
good
great
lovely
magnificent
mouth or nose
watering
outstanding
pretty
splendid
superior
superlative
tantalizing
triumphant

Beer Descriptors

Malt
malty
biscuit
rich
deep
slightly sweet
pale malty
roasty
cereal
oatmeal
cookie-like
caramel
roasty/toasty
burnt
burnt cream
scalded milk
bread-like
grainy
toffee-like
molasses-like
smoky
sweet
layered

Hops
fresh
floral
spring-like
spicy
earthy
citrusy
lemony
herbal
spruce-like
juniper-like
tangy
minty
piney

bitter
grassy
grapefruity
musty
sharp
bright
newly-mown lawn
grassy
pungent
aromatic

Yeast
yeasty
subtle
noticeable
pronounced
dominant
fresh-baked bread
clovelike
bubblegum
aromatic
tropical
fruity
clean
banana-like
earthy
musty

Conditioning
soft
effervescent
spritzy
sparkling
pinpoint
bubbly
gentle
low carbonation
highly carbonated

Body/Mouthfeel
dry
light
rich
creamy
full
heavy
oily
slick
thick
warm
thin
smooth
sweet
velvety

A NOTE FROM THE AUTHOR

Any suggestions, recommendations or new information intended to make this book more complete and user-friendly will be gratefully received and considered for inclusion in the next edition. And, of course, if you find anything in the book you believe to be inaccurate or misleading, I urge you to let me know. Please drop me an email message at michael.turback@gmail.com

Farm Fresh Books is an independently-owned specialty publisher of cookbooks and travel guides.

Our cookbooks celebrate the food, the people, and the mission of the nation's most enlightened public markets, farmers markets, and farm-to-table restaurants, capturing the grassroots connection to farms and fields and showcasing the bounty and enterprise of community gathering places.

Our travel guides examine what's new, what's enduring, and what's surprising in regional wine country. Thoughtfully-planned, easy-to-follow itineraries inspire and enrich visits to wineries, microbreweries, and along scenic and historic trails — making the most of a one-day jaunt or weekend excursion, including what to sip, where to eat, and where to stay.

Farm Fresh Books
www.farmfreshbooks.com